T0193075

IN THE DARK PLACES OF WISDOM

IN THE DARK
PLACES
OF
WISDOM

PETER KINGSLEY

First published in the United States in 1999 by
The Golden Sufi Center
P.O. Box 456, Point Reyes, California 94956.
www.goldensufi.org

Ninth printing 2023.

Printed and bound by Sheridan.

Kingsley, Peter.
    In the dark places of wisdom / Peter Kingsley.
        p.   cm.
    Includes bibliographical references.
    ISBN 1-890350-01-x (pbk.)
    1. Parmenides   I. Title.
B235.P24K56 1999
182'.3—dc21   98-12389
                                                                   CIP

ISBN 10: 1-890350-01-x
ISBN 13: 978-1-890350-01-7

Marseilles

CORSICA

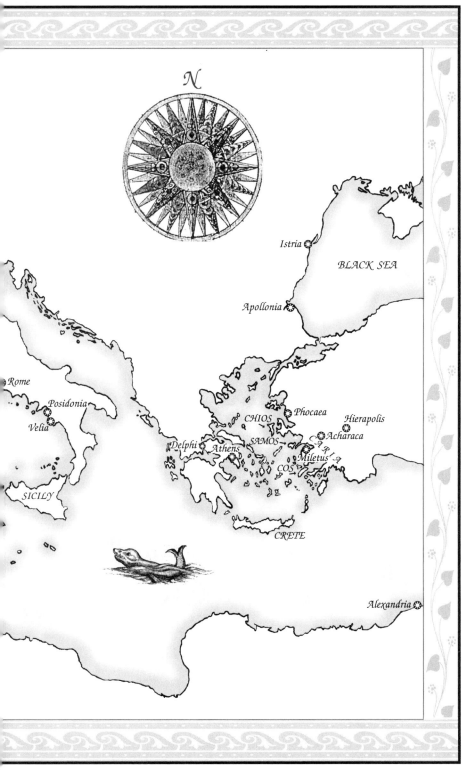

CONTENTS

ONE

This Book

T HIS BOOK IS NEITHER FACT NOR FICTION. IT'S about something stranger than both; and compared to that, what we call facts are just a fiction.

It's not what it seems, just as the things around us aren't what they seem. If you read on you'll see it's all about deception—about the total deception of the world we live in and about what lies behind.

It might seem to be a story about things that happened a long time ago. But really it's about ourselves. The details will probably be unfamiliar, very unfamiliar. And yet their significance reaches to the roots of our own being.

This unfamiliarity is important. Usually something is unfamiliar because it has no relation to us and we have no relation to it. But what's most unfamiliar of all is what's closest to us, and which we've forgotten. It's like a limb that's been anaesthetized or that's been unused for a long, long time. When we start feeling it again it's so strangely unfamiliar just because it's such an essential part of us.

And that's the purpose of this book: to awaken something we've forgotten, something we've been made to forget by the passing of time and by those who've misunderstood or—for reasons of their own—have wanted us to forget.

It could be said that this process of awakening is profoundly healing. It is. The only trouble with saying this is that we've come to have such a superficial idea of healing. For most of us, healing is what makes us comfortable and eases the pain. It's what softens, protects us. And yet what we want to be healed of is often what will heal us if we can stand the discomfort and the pain.

We want healing from illness, but it's through illness that we grow and are healed of our complacency. We're afraid of loss, and yet it's through what we lose that we're able to find what nothing can take away from us. We run from sadness and depression. But if we really face our sadness we find it speaks with the voice of our deepest longing; and if we face it a little longer we find that it teaches us the way to attain what we long for.

And what is it that we long for? That's what this story is about.

Our Ancestors

I F YOU'RE LUCKY, AT SOME POINT IN YOUR LIFE you'll come to a complete dead end.

Or to put it another way: if you're lucky you'll come to a crossroads and see that the path to the left leads to hell, that the path to the right leads to hell, that the road straight ahead leads to hell and that if you try to turn around you'll end up in complete and utter hell.

Every way leads to hell and there's no way out, nothing left for you to do. Nothing can possibly satisfy you any more. Then, if you're ready, you'll start to discover inside yourself what you always longed for but were never able to find.

And if you're not lucky?

If you're not lucky you'll only come to this point when you die. And that won't be a pretty sight because you'll still be wanting what you're no longer able to have. We are human beings, endowed with an incredible dignity; but there's nothing more undignified than forgetting our greatness and clutching at straws.

This life of the senses can never fulfil us, even though the whole world will tell us the opposite. It never was meant to fulfil us. The truth is so simple, so lovingly simple: if we want to grow up, become true men and women, we have to face death before we die. We have to discover what it is to be able to slide behind the scenes and disappear.

Our western culture carefully keeps us from such things. It keeps going, and thriving, by persuading us to value everything that's unimportant. And that's why over the past hundred years so many people have turned away, turned to the East, anywhere—for some form of spiritual nourishment, for a taste of something else. At first it was the great religions of the East; now it's small tribes and hidden cultures.

But we belong to the West. The more we find in the East or anywhere else the more it makes us inwardly divided, homeless in our own land. We become cultural tramps and vagabonds. The solutions we find are never fundamental answers. They only create more problems.

AND YET THERE'S SOMETHING we were never told.

Even in these modern times, what half-heartedly is described as mystical perception is always pushed to the periphery. When it's not denied it's held at arm's length—

out there at the margins of society. But what we haven't been told is that a spiritual tradition lies at the very roots of western civilization.

You could say the people concerned were mystics. But they weren't mystics as we might understand mystics: that idea of mysticism only came into being much later.

They were intensely practical—so practical that, thousands of years ago, they sowed the seeds of western culture and shaped the structure of the world we live in. To the extent that we take part in the culture of this western world, they're our ancestors. Now we struggle around in what they created, oblivious of our past.

Almost singlehandedly they laid the foundation for disciplines that were to make the West what it now is: chemistry, physics, astronomy, biology, rhetoric, logic. But they did all this with an understanding we no longer have, because their knowledge came from a wisdom that to us is no more than a myth.

And it's not just that they've been misunderstood. That's only a small part of it. They also knew they would be misunderstood. They realized they were dealing with children who would walk away with the pieces that took their fancy and fail to see the whole.

And so it came about. Nothing about who those people were, or what they taught, is appreciated any more. Even the traces of their existence have almost been wiped out. Their names are hardly known to anyone.

Fragments of what they said are kept in the hands of a few scholars, who do just what Jesus described. They hold the keys of knowledge but hide them; and they don't go in themselves or open the doors for anyone else.

But behind those doors is something we can no longer do without. The gifts we were given don't work any more, and we threw away the instructions for how to use them a long time ago.

Now it's important to make contact with that tradition again—not just for our sakes but for the sake of something larger. It's important because there's no other way forward. And we don't have to look outside ourselves. We don't have to turn to a culture any different from the world we live in. Everything we need is inside us, deep in our own roots, just waiting to be touched.

And yet for contact with that tradition a price has to be paid. A price always has to be paid, and it's because people weren't willing to pay the price that things have ended up the way they have.

The price is what it always has been: ourselves, our willingness to be transformed. Nothing less will do.

We can't just stand back and watch. We can't stand back because we ourselves are the missing ingredient. Without our involvement words are only words. And that tradition didn't exist to edify, or entertain, or even to inspire. It existed to draw people home.

So it's good to know what's involved. This isn't a book to satisfy your curiosity or create more curiosity. It's about men who took everything away from the people they taught and gave them nothing that can be imagined in return.

To most of us this will sound like craziness, sheer nonsense. And that's exactly what it is, because it comes from beyond the senses. It just so happens to be the same nonsense that gave rise to the western world—a nonsense so powerful but so elusive that people have tried for thousands of years to make sense of it, and always failed.

SO MANY OF US today are concerned about the extinction of all the species that the western world is wiping out. But there's hardly anyone who notices the most extraordinary threat of all: the extinction of our knowledge of what we are.

For we're not just twenty or forty or seventy years old. That's only an appearance. We're ancient, incredibly ancient. We hold the history of the stars in our pockets.

That knowledge that's gone missing has to do with the past. And yet it has nothing to do with the past as we understand the past. We are the past. Even our tomorrows are the past acting itself out. We like to think we can step into the future by leaving the past behind, but that can't be done. We only move into the future when we turn to face our past and become what we are.

So let's start at the beginning—with the people who were ancestors of our ancestors.

Phocaea

THEY WERE TRADERS, EXPLORERS, PIRATES. Those who have studied them call them the Vikings of antiquity. They were the most daring adventurers among the ancient Greeks, pushing at the frontiers of the unknown. What others dreamed of they converted into reality.

They were called Phocaeans, and the name of their town was Phocaea. It was a small place perched on the west coast of what's now known as Turkey, just a little to the north of what's now the city of Izmir.

From this home of theirs they became famous for pushing out to the west beyond the point where most Greeks thought it was possible for humans to go. Old traditions say they were the first to travel out on a regular basis beyond Gibraltar into the Atlantic; that was in the seventh and sixth centuries BC. It was colonists from Phocaea who sailed down the west coast of Africa, and then up to France and England, to Scotland and beyond.

And there was the east. Phocaea's position was a privileged one. It stood close to the western end of the great caravan route that stretched for thousands of miles, from the Mediterranean through Anatolia and Syria down towards the Persian Gulf. This was the famous Royal Road: the route that was used for centuries by the kings of western Asia and of Persia, then by Alexander the Great—and, much later, by the Christians to spread their message to the West. It brought oriental influences in art and religion through to the western world even before Phocaea became famous, and it carried Greek influence back the other way. It made Phocaea a key point in the contact between ancient East and West.

PHOCAEA means 'city of seals'. The Phocaeans themselves were amphibians, always focused on the ocean. They wrote most of their history in water—and the sea doesn't leave many traces.

So it's good to look around. That can help to give a better feel for the type of world they used to live in: a world still forgotten and almost unknown. Don't worry about any of the detail. It's not important in itself. Just let it spread out in front of you like a peacock's tail and watch the eyes looking back at you. For this isn't someone else's history; it's your own.

There's Samos—an island a little to the south of Phocaea, just off the mainland of Asia. Samos and Phocaea had a lot in common. The Phocaeans were the specialists of specialists in long-distance trade, but the people of Samos were also famous for exactly the same thing. Phocaeans and Samians both had a reputation that was almost mythical in its dimensions for trading with Andalusia and the distant west. Remarkable discoveries made in Spain, and on Samos, bear their reputations out.

Then there was Egypt. It wouldn't be fair to say that people from Samos or Phocaea simply did business with Egypt. They did much more: they built their own depots and places of worship along the Nile, together with other Greeks. For Samians, or Phocaeans, Egypt wasn't just some foreign land. It was part of the world they knew and lived and worked in.

Samos was the home of Pythagoras. At any rate it was his home until he sailed west and settled in Italy, around 530 BC. The stories passed down from century to century in the ancient world were that Pythagoras learned his wisdom by travelling to Egypt and Andalusia; to Phoenicia, a region roughly similar to the coastal areas of Lebanon and Syria; to Persia, Babylonia, India.

Nowadays scholars like to laugh at such stories. They dismiss them as romantic fantasies, projected back onto a famous Greek islander by later Greeks who wanted to invent early connections between western culture and the East. But it's better to be a little more careful.

According to an old tradition Pythagoras' father was a gem engraver. If you look closely at the tradition you'll see there are excellent reasons to accept it as true. And what Pythagoras' father did, Pythagoras himself will have learned: as a matter of course in those days he will have been brought up to follow his father's trade. But for a Greek gem engraver of the time, in the middle of the sixth century BC, life will have meant certain things. It will have meant learning skills introduced from Phoenicia, and buying in materials from the East. It's no surprise that later Greek writers say Pythagoras' own father was a trader between Samos and Phoenicia.

There used to be another tradition about Pythagoras: a tradition based on the best of sources. It says he used to wear trousers. That's very strange. Greeks didn't wear trousers; only Persians and Iranian people did. But to start making sense of the tradition we just have to look at another man from Samos—a man called Theodorus.

Theodorus lived at the time of Pythagoras and Pythagoras' father. He was a gem engraver, and a fine sculptor and architect as well. Ancient writers say he worked and learned in Egypt; recent findings from Egypt have helped dramatically to confirm what they say.

We also know other things about Theodorus. We know how he worked personally for kings of western Anatolia—what now is the western part of Turkey—and for the king of Persia. There are good reasons to link him with some of the finest architecture produced right in the heart of ancient Persia itself.

That could seem extraordinary. In a sense it is. But Theodorus, like Pythagoras, came from Samos: an island that from century to century had the closest of links with Persia in trade, diplomacy, art.

And Theodorus wasn't alone. By chance we happen to know of another Greek sculptor who worked for two generations of Persian kings, a long way away from his home. His name was Telephanes. He wasn't from Samos but from Phocaea.

DIFFERENT PEOPLE make journeys for different reasons. Sometimes they're forced; sometimes they think they choose.

But what's important is that long-distance travel happened, and happened on a large scale. It was far more common in the ancient world than we've been led to believe, just as it was in the Middle Ages. And what's most striking of all is that even when Greece was at the height of war with Persia and you'd least expect it, intelligent Greeks streamed out to Persia to learn, make money, find wiser people.

Artists and craftsmen settled there together with their families; by pooling their resources they helped to build up the Persian empire. Long before, the Greek arts of stone carving had been shaped and influenced by the East. Now it was Greeks who shaped the greatest achievements of Persian architecture.

And yet that's still just a small part of the story. The best scholars have come to realize something rather hard to admit. Pythagoras' most famous discoveries really weren't his discoveries at all. They were already known for centuries in Babylonia, and the most that Pythagoras can be credited for is bringing the knowledge of them to Greece and adapting them to the world of the Greeks. But even the scholars who've realized this haven't seen how effortlessly Pythagoras' home island explains the link with Babylonia.

The greatest temple on Samos was dedicated to Hera, mother of the gods. It was famous throughout the Greek world. During the sixth century BC it was vastly enlarged and rebuilt; the new design was based on Egyptian models.

And inside the sacred precincts of the temple strange bronze objects have been found. The objects had already been left there even earlier, in the seventh century, as dedications. They're strange from the point of view of the Greeks—but they're well known from the East.

They're images that belonged to the cult of Gula, the Babylonian goddess of healing. And they didn't arrive in Samos simply because of trade. They arrived there because religion and worship crossed the boundaries of countries, ignored the limits of language. It was just the same with art. Artists on Samos copied Babylonian cult images, imitated the features of Babylonian demons.

Oriental imports poured into Samos out of Syria and Babylonia, from the seventh through to the fifth centuries BC. Foreign traders arrived from the East. But the opposite also happened: Samians travelled out east themselves, and the trade routes stayed busy down to the time of Pythagoras.

Where there's movement of goods and objects the way is open for travel. Where the paths of cultural contact exist there's a standing invitation for the seeker. That should be obvious; at any rate it used to be. 'Trade' and 'inquiry'—these were two terms the Greeks loved to group together because they knew they went hand in hand.

And as for Hera's temple, it didn't only become the home for imports from Babylonia or Egypt or Persia. It was also a storehouse for objects brought in from Andalusia and Phoenicia, from the Caucasus, from Central Asia. And one of the imports stayed beautifully alive. Peacocks were introduced into all of the western world from the temple of Hera on Samos. They were bred in the temple grounds and treated as sacred to the goddess.

They were carried to Samos, through Persia, from India.

THE SIXTH CENTURY WENT BY and Babylon became part of the Persian empire. But not much really changed at all: Babylonia, Persia and India had had the closest of ties for ages. Now there were just more reasons to travel. In Babylonia you would meet natives from Mesopotamia, you would meet Persians, and you would find whole communities of Indians.

Settlements of Greeks lived there too, Greeks who had been working and trading in Babylon since the start of the century. They were direct forerunners of the Greek communities that would go on living there for another seven hundred years. And among those earlier settlers were people from one particular area in Anatolia—an area called Caria. When the Persian king wanted India explored by experienced people he could trust, he chose a man from Caria. There'll be more things to say about Carians later, and their links with Phocaea.

For a long time we've been told to believe that the ancient Greeks were a self-enclosed people, unwilling to learn foreign languages, creating western civilization all on their own. We haven't quite been told the truth. The links with the East were there to begin with, behind everything that was to occur and has occurred since then.

It's good to bear this in mind.

THE TIME: AROUND 540 BC.

Something happened in Phocaea. You could hardly say it was unexpected. The Phocaeans had guessed for a long while that some day it would happen. They had even been given a small fortune by their trading partners in the Atlantic so they could build a protective wall. But there are some things you can do nothing to change, even when you see them coming in advance.

The people of Phocaea had done trade with Persia for years. They would also go on doing so for years to come. At any rate those of them would who eventually found their way back to the town and kept it going as a kind of shadow of what it once had been.

Right now, though, the situation had changed. For religious and political and economic reasons—but ultimately everything came down to religion—Persia wanted to extend its empire to the ends of the earth. The Persians were thirsty. They no longer wanted to do business with Phocaea. They wanted Phocaea.

The army had arrived. The commander delivered his ultimatum: accept my terms or die. And no amount of protective walls was going to be of any use. The Persians had learned a trick and knew how to climb over them by building up mounds of earth outside.

Pinned between the wall and the sea, the people of Phocaea came up with a trick of their own. They asked to have the night to think things over. The Persian commander said he knew what they were up to but wouldn't interfere. Sometimes the wisest course of all is to allow others to trick you.

They gathered whatever they could. They took everything down to their ships: their families, all their movable possessions. They took the images and sacred objects from the temples, everything they were able to carry; the heavy bronzework, stone carvings and paintings were all they left behind. And they set sail.

They had escaped death, and surrender, at least for the moment. And the Persians took possession of an empty town.

The next step was to find a new home. They asked their neighbours on the island of Chios if they could buy a few small islands from them—islands scattered between Chios and the Asiatic mainland. The Chians refused. They knew how good the Phocaeans were at business and had no intention of encouraging competition on their doorstep.

Once again it was time to go. But now it was time to leave the part of the world they'd grown up and lived in.

First they swore an oath—all of them. They threw some iron in the sea and promised none of them would ever return to Phocaea until the iron floated on the surface. It's an old oath, shared by East and West. You still find Chinese love poets swearing the same way centuries later: 'We promised to love until iron floats on the river.'

THEY AGREED to sail west, to Corsica.

Corsica was an obvious choice. A few of the Phocaeans had already left home and founded a colony there some twenty years earlier. Founding a colony was a serious business in those days, and it was normal to ask the oracle of the god Apollo at Delphi about where to go. Apollo might answer with a riddle: he usually did. But the answer was what mattered.

So people had gone from Phocaea to Delphi to ask for advice, and Apollo had suggested they build a town on Cyrnus. At least that's what they thought he'd suggested. Cyrnus was a Greek name for Corsica and that's where they'd decided to go.

Now, twenty years later, the Phocaeans were agreeing for a second time to sail to Corsica. But this time the agreement wasn't strong enough. In spite of the Persians, in spite of the oath about the iron and the sea, around half the people just couldn't go. It was simply too painful to leave everything behind: the longing for their home was too great. They made their way back and bowed to the Persians, weighed down by the curse of their broken oath.

The rest of them did set sail. And when at last they arrived in Corsica they were welcomed by the original settlers from Phocaea. They all lived together for several years; built new temples to house the sacred objects they'd brought with them.

And the good times didn't last. There were too many of them now, with much too little to live off. So they did what they knew best—turned to piracy. It wasn't long before their victims had had enough and joined forces to destroy them in a battle at sea.

The Phocaeans didn't stand a chance. They were massively outnumbered. But they won. The only problem was that, as so often happens, in winning they almost destroyed themselves. They lost so many ships and ruined so many others, lost so many men for one reason or another, that there was no way they could stay on and risk another attack.

Again they were homeless; but this time things were different. The oracle at Delphi had advised the Phocaeans to build a home on Cyrnus. They had done exactly what Apollo said and been almost totally destroyed. Nothing made sense any more. There was no one to guide them, tell them where to go. They started drifting back south the way they'd come, and eastwards until they arrived at a town right on the tip of the bottom of Italy. And they stopped.

It was then they met the man who changed everything. He was just a stranger. He came from a place called Posidonia, back some way up the western coast of Italy. But he put all their doubts to rest.

'You got everything wrong', the stranger said. 'You thought Apollo told you to build a place on Cyrnus; but that's only what you thought. What he was really telling you all those years ago was to build a place for Cyrnus.'

What the stranger meant was quite simple, once you understood it. Cyrnus may have been a name for Corsica but it was also the name of a mythical hero, a hero who had been the son of the greatest hero of all time—Heracles. The 'on' and the 'for': they're different words in English, but ancient Greek was much more compact. One word in Greek often meant the same as two or three words in another language. It easily allowed for double meanings, even in everyday talk.

And yet there was one form of the language that was most famous of all, even to the Greeks, for its ambiguities and double meanings. That was the language of oracles. When gods spoke through oracles they spoke in a way that's hard for humans to understand. The hardness is what makes the difference between the human and the divine.

The Phocaeans took the stranger's hint. He had set them free from their confusion—free from the limitations of place, of 'here' and 'there'. Life was still waiting for them, waiting to be lived. Everything had seemed so hopeless. But all they had done was interpret the oracle too narrowly, understand it on the physical level instead of at the level of myth.

They did build a place. They built it close to the stranger's hometown of Posidonia. They settled, and lived there for centuries. And they changed what the world was to become. The name of their town was spelt and spoken in different ways by different people: Hyele, Elea, Velia.

We'll call it Velia.

Fairy Story

T HAT'S THE STORY OF THE FOUNDING OF VELIA, more or less as it was told by the man often called the father of western history: Herodotus.

He's also known as the father of lies. He was already being called that by Greeks two thousand years ago. So is this story of the founding of Velia true, or a fiction? It sounds like a novel, almost a fairy story.

Nowadays historians argue with alarming passion about how much or how little we can trust the stories he wrote. But if it's the wanderings of Phocaeans—or Samians—that we're concerned with then we're rather lucky. Modern archaeologists who have dug the earth and searched in places mentioned by Herodotus have been struck by how precisely the things they find confirm what Herodotus said.

So what about the lies?

Well, first we have to understand some basic things. Writers in ancient Greece weren't concerned with truth and lies in quite the same way we are. The approval for truth, the disapproval for lies: they're something that only evolved very gradually to become what they are. Lies weren't just the opposite of honesty or the denial of truth. They had their own reality, their own function.

At the time when Herodotus was writing, in the fifth century BC, it was still assumed that the best writers wrote through inspiration—divine inspiration. Those who were inspired were inspired by the Muses and the Muses were like other gods. They weren't limited by truth, or honesty; it was their divine right to lie most of the time and be truthful if they wanted. That's because for the ancient Greeks truth and lies existed side by side, went hand in hand. One was connected to the other deep inside their being. And the more someone tried to insist he was just telling the truth, the more his listeners or readers would laugh inwardly and assume he was trying to trick them. Things were a little different in those days.

And then there's another question: the question of who we are to decide what are the truths and what are the lies. It's so easy to think we have superior knowledge, that our understanding is better. We love to correct the errors of the past in terms of what we now think is true. But who's going to correct our errors? Everyone used to know that the sun goes round the earth; now everyone believes they know that the earth goes round the sun. The trouble is that every great step in understanding always demolishes and overturns the knowledge that went before. People will only look back on us in the way we look back at the past.

There's no real wisdom in any of this. The one thing worth doing is to get behind it all, to the essential that never changes.

THAT STRANGER from Posidonia, was he real? The theme of the helpful stranger, who suddenly appears and rescues you from your troubles, is something we're all familiar with from stories and tales. So is it just a fiction, a lie? Or did the theme come into being because these helpful strangers—whose helpfulness has a quality that verges on the divine—used to exist?

We could break our heads open trying to find answers to questions like these. But sometimes the facts are simple. The fact is that there used to be men just like him in southern Italy: men who really existed. They were called 'the wise' because their wisdom verged on the divine; because they were able to see beyond the surface and behind appearances; because they were able to interpret oracles and dreams and the riddles of existence. Some of them came to be known as Pythagoreans—people who lived in the spirit of Pythagoras.

And the oracles from Delphi: they too were real, and really were given to people who wanted to create colonies. Men used to live by them. Sometimes they died by them when they got them wrong. Just because oracles were ambiguous you always took a risk. You could never be quite sure exactly how things would turn out. It would be much the same as if we were to live our lives now guided by the dreams we have in the night. There's no security in that, none at all. It's not for those of us who want to live a safe life—or at least what we imagine is a safe life, cushioned by our modern myths.

Oracles are never what they seem. For oracles to be oracles they have to contain something hidden. The more you think you understand them the less you probably do. That's where the danger lies. As ancient Greeks said, the words spoken by oracles are like seeds. They contain a fullness, a pregnancy of meaning, dimensions of relevance that only become apparent with time. Human language is like a splinter: fragmented, isolated, sticking out in one direction. But the language of the gods is full of surprises that surround you from all directions and jump out on you from behind.

That's what happened with the Delphic oracle as interpreted by the stranger from Posidonia. By directing the Phocaeans away from Cyrnus the island to Cyrnus the hero he did something very specific—something very important to understand.

To the Greeks, founding a colony was closely bound up with oracles; but it was also bound up with heroes. The first people who ever founded colonies were the heroes from the mythical past. And if you wanted to found a colony then heroes were your prototype: the hero held in his hand the mythical map for you to use and follow. So by pointing the Phocaeans away from the island to the hero, the man from Posidonia was pointing them straight to the roots of their own endeavour. He was directing them back into the heroic dimension, reconnecting them in their role as colonizers with their mythical source.

IT'S NO COINCIDENCE that the man from Posidonia interpreted the oracle as referring to a son of Heracles.

Posidonia and the region around it, along with the rest of southern Italy, were the land of Heracles. This was the land he had once travelled, where he had experienced his mythical adventures and ordeals. Now Posidonia and the neighbouring areas were steeped in heroic tradition. The cults of Heracles and other heroes were more alive here than anywhere else. Stories of heroic experiences—like Heracles' descent to the underworld—were central themes of the local religion, unforgettable parts of people's daily lives. It's no accident that Herodotus talks about a son of Heracles while mentioning a town immersed in the knowledge of everything to do with Heracles.

And there's more. When you look at those 'wise men' of southern Italy who were famous in their time for understanding oracles and looking behind the scenes of existence, you find something very particular.

You find that to them heroes weren't just figures in some mythical past. For them the heroic ideal was something that had to be lived in the present. The aim of one's life, the life of a wise man, was to follow the way of the hero—to live his ordeals, his sufferings, his transformation. That's what provided the spiritual purpose and the map of their existence. You can still see how this imitation of the hero was adapted by Christianity to become the imitation of Christ.

Just how it was that the ideal of the hero also came to be lived at Velia, and just how it happened that traditions of heroes and oracles went on living there hand in hand: we'll come to that later.

But here, in this spiral of meanings and implications, there's one basic point to bear in mind. The founding of Velia wasn't what historians now like to make it—simply a matter of ships sailing into a harbour and houses and walls being built. When the Phocaeans settled in their new home it was because of oracles and heroes that they settled there. Apollo and a son of Heracles, heroes and oracles: those were the crucial factors behind the founding of the town of Velia.

VELIA became an important city. Its foundation was a major event in the history of the ancient Greeks and the history of the West. But it wasn't the only new town seeded by the Phocaeans in the sixth century BC.

They also created a town called Massalia, a little further on to the west. You'll have heard of it by its later name: Marseilles.

Marseilles still exists. Velia disappeared a long time ago; until recently hardly anyone even knew where the town once used to be. And yet Velia still lives on in a way that's now almost impossible to understand, because its influence on the West has been so profound. The real origins of western philosophy, of so many ideas that shaped the world we live in, lie in Velia.

You may think you know what I mean by philosophy. It's very unlikely that you do. Centuries have been spent destroying the truth about what it once was. We only have eyes now for what philosophy has become—no idea of what it no longer is.

The basic meaning of philosophy is love of wisdom. That means very little any more. We have plenty of room in our lives for knowledge and data, for learning and information, amusement and entertainment; but not for wisdom.

This is how things are now. And yet they weren't always like that. We can still trace out how, well over two thousand years ago, the schools of Plato and Aristotle put the seal on what was to become the most enduring Athenian contribution to intellectual history in the West: instead of the love of wisdom, philosophy turned into the love of talking and arguing about the love of wisdom. Since then the talking and arguing have pushed everything else out of the picture—until now we no longer know of anything else or can even imagine that there could be.

But we're concerned with the period before then, with what happened before the people who achieved this. For their lives were the deaths of the people we're concerned with.

What's Missing

WHAT ISN'T THERE, IN FRONT OF OUR EYES, IS usually more real than what is.

We can see that at every level of existence.

Even when we're finally where we want to be—with the person we love, with the things we struggled for—our eyes are still on the horizon. They're still on where to go next, what to do next, what we want the person we love to do and be. If we just stay where we are in the present moment, seeing what we're seeing and hearing what we're hearing and forgetting everything else, we feel we're about to die; and our mind tortures us until we think of something else to live for. We have to keep finding a way away from where we are, into what we imagine is the future.

What's missing is more powerful than what's there in front of our eyes. We all know that. The only trouble is that the missingness is too hard to bear, so we invent things to miss in our desperation. They are all only temporary substitutes. The world fills us with substitute after substitute and tries to convince us that nothing is missing. But nothing has the power to fill the hollowness we feel inside, so we have to keep replacing and modifying the things we invent as our emptiness throws its shadow over our life.

You can see the same thing quite often with people who never knew their father. The unknown father casts an enchanted spell across the whole of their existence, touching every corner. They're always just about to find him in the form of something or someone. They never do.

And you can see it with people who love the divine, or God—who miss what doesn't even exist for anyone else. With people who want this or that, there's always the risk that their wanting will be fulfilled. But when you want what's so much greater than yourself there's never a chance of being finally fulfilled. And yet something very strange happens. When you want that and refuse to settle for anything else, it comes to you. People who love the divine go around with holes in their hearts, and inside the hole is the universe. It's people like them that this book is about.

And there's a great secret: we all have that vast missingness deep inside us. The only difference between us and the mystics is that they learn to face what we find ways of running away from. That's the reason why mysticism has been pushed to the periphery of our culture: because the more we feel that nothingness inside us, the more we feel the need to fill the void. So we try to substitute this and that, but nothing lasts. We keep wanting something else, needing some other need to keep us going—until we come to the point of our death and find ourselves still wanting the thousand substitutes we're no longer able to have.

Western culture is a past master at the art of substitution. It offers and never delivers because it can't. It has lost the power even to know what needs to be delivered, so it offers substitutes instead. What's most important is missing, and dazzling in its absence. And what we're offered is often just a substitute for something far finer that once used to exist, or still does exist, but has nothing in common with it except the name.

Even religion and spirituality and humanity's higher aspirations become wonderful substitutes. And that's what happened to philosophy. What used to be ways to freedom for our ancestors become prisons and cages for us. We create schemes and structures, and climb up and down inside them. But these are just monkey tricks and parlour games to console us and distract us from the longing in our hearts.

When you turn away from all the substitutes there's suddenly no future any more, just the present. There's nowhere to go, and that's the ultimate terror for the mind. But if you can stay in this hell, with no way to the left or to the right or in front or behind, then you discover the peace of utter stillness—the stillness at the heart of this story.

≋

THERE'S ONE MAN who influenced the western world in a way no one else did. He lies buried under our thoughts, under all our ideas and theories. And the world he belonged to is buried there too: a feminine world of incredible beauty and depth and power and wisdom, a world so close to us that we've forgotten where to find it.

To a few specialists he's known as 'the central problem' in making sense of what happened to philosophy before Plato. And there's no coming to grips with the history of philosophy or wisdom in the West without understanding him. He lies on the central nerve of our culture. Touch him, and indirectly you're in touch with everything else.

He's said to have created the idea of metaphysics. It's said that he invented logic: the basis of our reasoning, the foundation of every single discipline that has come into existence in the West.

His influence on Plato was immense. There's a well-known saying that the whole history of western philosophy is just a series of footnotes to Plato. With the same justification Plato's philosophy in its developed form could be called a series of footnotes to that man.

And yet it's claimed that we know next to nothing about him. This is hardly surprising. Plato and his disciple Aristotle have become the great names, the intellectual heroes of our culture. But one of the drawbacks of creating heroes is that the taller we make them stand the longer the shadows they cast—and the more they're allowed to conceal and push into the dark.

In fact we know a great deal about him, but without knowing it yet. Life is kind. It gives us what we need just when we most need it. Extraordinary things were discovered about him a little while ago: discoveries more amazing than most pieces of fiction. But scholars still refuse to understand the evidence or its significance—even though the discoveries only confirm what should already have been clear for thousands of years from the evidence that's been available for so long.

The problem is that all this evidence forces us to start understanding ourselves, and our past, in a very different way. The easiest solution has been to silence it and cover it up. But there are things that can only be silenced for so long.

We could talk about many other things. We could talk about other people in the history of early Greek philosophy, and how a picture of them has been created that bears no similarity to the realities: about how they've been reshaped and rationalized to bring them into line with the interests of our times. We could talk about how profoundly those people have been misunderstood through the failure to take into account the closeness of their links with traditions of the East—traditions that have hardly begun to be taken seriously. And we could talk about how the western scourge of believing ourselves superior to other civilizations grew out of the need to compensate for our immense indebtedness to the East. We could also talk about how some of those so-called philosophers were magicians. And we will.

But these are all just secondary issues. There's so much of our own history that needs to be rewritten; and yet what's most important of all is to know where to start. Almost everything that's thought certain and sure about early western philosophy is unsure, and will become even more insecure as the years go by. But in the middle of all these uncertainties there's one firm piece of ground—the existence of that man whose fundamental importance in shaping the history of western ideas is beyond denying.

With him we have a solid grip on what really happened deep in our past. Understand him, and we're in a position to start understanding many other things.

His name was Parmenides. He was from Velia.

Killing the Father

THE OLDEST DESCRIPTIONS OF PARMENIDES ARE strange ones. They're like markers on his grave. It's good to look at them first because they say so much about what happened to him.

Plato wrote a dialogue about him. It's called *Parmenides*. It presents him at Athens as a very old man, white-haired, arguing about philosophical issues in the presence of a very young man—Plato's teacher Socrates.

Plato manages to be carefully vague about just how old Parmenides was at the time of the debate: 'around sixty-five or something like that'. But that was old enough to present him as a man whose time is past. For ancient Greeks the age of sixty was a reasonable time to die.

If you wanted to take seriously the hints in Plato's dialogue about age and date and time, you could work out that Parmenides would have been born around 520 or 515 BC. And yet there's a problem. The whole of the *Parmenides* is a deliberate fiction. It has Parmenides debate abstract Platonic theories in a way he never could have or would have: what Plato describes never happened.

It brings Parmenides' successor, Zeno, into the debate only to undermine him and belittle him. It has him discredit his own writings in front of everyone; makes Parmenides coolly distance himself from him. And after emphasizing what a very handsome and well-proportioned man Zeno was, Plato keeps bringing up a rumour that he was Parmenides' young lover as a way of compromising his position even more: one of the best-loved topics for gossip and innuendo in Plato's own Athenian circle was that if a pupil seems close to his teacher then sex is bound to be at the bottom of it all.

From beginning to end the setting of the *Parmenides* is skilfully designed with one purpose in mind. That's to present Socrates and Plato—not Zeno or anyone else— as the legitimate heirs to Parmenides' teaching.

This is nothing to be surprised at. It was a well-recognized principle in the circle of people close to Plato: rearrange the past to suit your purposes, put ideas of your own into the mouths of famous figures from the past, have no concern for historical details. And Plato himself had no scruples about inventing the most elaborate fictions, about recreating history, altering people's ages, moving dates around.

All that's surprising is how normal it's become to take him seriously when we shouldn't—and not take him seriously when we should.

BUT IT'S NOT JUST that his dialogues aren't historical documents, or that he would have laughed at us for wanting to think they are. There's more to the matter than that.

Plato was writing early in the fourth century BC. Then time had just started to solidify around the Greeks and around what was to become of the West. Before, history had been what lived in your blood—what related to your ancestors. Individual towns or cities could keep their own careful records of the passing of the years; but that was strictly a matter of local concern. Now something else was happening. History was being structured into universal facts and figures. Mythology was changing into chronology.

When the Greeks of his time looked behind them into the fifth century and beyond they were looking into a realm of myth, of local traditions that reached back to a world of gods and heroes. Plato was living in a period when writing about the past was still a matter of free enterprise. History as we know it was only just being made.

We have so little sense for the past, or for the history of time. When we manage to keep an appointment and get there on time we imagine we're up with the moment.

But what we don't see is that the time on the clock is ancient. Our divisions of the day into hours or minutes or seconds are Babylonian and Egyptian inventions. Our time is steeped in the past; we live and die in the past. Now even scientists understand that time isn't a fixed reality outside us.

Greek historians in the centuries after Plato started making it their business to sound as accurate as possible about what happened in the past—just as we do. But with them things weren't what they appeared to be, just as they aren't now; and the greater their apparent precision the greater their guesses. Some of them made Parmenides' birth date coincide exactly with the year of the founding of Velia. It was only a guess.

There's no precise or reliable dating for Parmenides that survives. We just have rough indications; but they're good enough. The indications are that he was born not that long after the Phocaeans arrived in southern Italy on their journey from the east—that he was among the first generation of children brought up by Phocaean parents in Velia, with the memories of Phocaea and of the journey from Phocaea still running fresh in their blood.

IN ANOTHER of his fictional dialogues Plato has Socrates describe the figure of Parmenides.

He seemed to me—to quote from Homer—someone 'worthy of my reverence and awe'. I spent some time in the man's company when I was very young and he was very old, and he gave me the impression of possessing a certain depth that was noble through and through. This makes me all the more afraid not just that we won't understand what he said but that we'll fail to a far greater extent to understand what it is he meant.

The picture is impressive; and yet there's nothing straightforward here at all. The words are full of praise. But as so often in Plato, they're double-edged. The quotation from Homer raises Parmenides to the rank of an ancient hero, straight out of mythology. The trouble is that these were the words spoken by Helen to the great lord Priam —the ruler of Troy who was soon to be destroyed along with his kingdom.

When Socrates mentions the time he spent in Parmenides' company he sounds convincing enough. But he's just referring back to the imaginary meeting in the *Parmenides*: one fiction referring to another. And as for his fear of not understanding Parmenides' words or meaning, the statement seems sincere. In fact it's a skilful technique—Plato's way of giving himself the freedom he needs to start interpreting Parmenides as he wants.

But the impression of Parmenides' inner depth: that's something to remember.

THERE'S ANOTHER PLACE where Plato talks about Parmenides. You'd hardly think it was significant. No one really does.

In a third dialogue Plato chooses his speakers with care. His concern is still very clear. It's to present his teaching, once again, as the legitimate successor to the tradition of philosophy that began in Velia. And there's one point where he makes his characters see just what has to be done to establish the line of succession. The main speaker says: we're going to have to resort to violence against our 'father' Parmenides. We're going to have to kill the father.

Plato deliberately steps around the issue, states it without really stating it; makes it sound casual, almost a joke. But we have to understand one thing. For Plato jokes are hardly ever just jokes. What for him is most serious appears as a game, and when he treats something with humour is often when there's most at stake. That's a part of what makes him engaging: it was appreciated very well in the ancient world, and it was appreciated in the Renaissance. He loved trying to catch his readers out by stating the most serious things in the most light-hearted ways.

And there's something else as well. In the ancient world you never joked about patricide. The whole of

44

Greek society revolved around the relationship between father and son. Any act of violence at all against your father was the greatest crime there was—not to mention killing him. Patricide was about the most appalling crime that could be imagined. Even the word 'patricide' was a word best never pronounced at all. Gods could kill their fathers; but when humans were involved it became a crime of mythological dimensions.

What is it that Plato killed? That's what we'll begin to discover in this book. And to see what Parmenides was is to see why Plato had to kill him. For if he hadn't done what he did, the West as we know it would never have existed.

Plato had to commit patricide, get Parmenides out of the way. And the murder was so complete that now we don't even know it ever happened, or what was killed.

The only way we can suspect what happened is when we feel something missing inside. For what Parmenides represented: no one can ever get that out of the way. It will always find its way back. We can do without it for a while, but only for a while.

Two

ἣ δ᾽ ἄρ᾽ ἔριμνον ἐφ᾽ αἱματαμαχαῖς τ᾽ ἄρμα καὶ ἵπποισιν. καί με
θεᾶ περίφρων ὑπεδέξατο. χαῖρε ἠ χειρί εἰδότη τ όφρα μὴ
ἔχειν. ὃ δὲ δὴ ἔπος φάθ᾽. καί με περισσῶς δαι· ὢ
κοῦ ἐὰ θανάτου σῖ σῶ αἰδὼς κ᾽ ἡ υἱός χοισίν. ἵππω δαῖ
φθόνου οὖν· ἱκανῶν ἡ μυθρρι δὰ᾽ χαῖ ρὲ πᾶ χ᾽ π σεμόῖρ
κακὴ προ᾽ ὑ πόμπημε νεσθ᾽. τὴν δὲ δ᾽ ἡ τὰ ἀπ᾽ ὤν
θρώπων ἱμπᾶς πό του ἵ. ἀλλὰ θέμις τε δίκη τε· χρεὼ

Getting Started

P ARMENIDES WROTE A POEM.

It would be easy to imagine the father of philosophy producing very different things. But he just wrote a poem.

He wrote it in the metre of the great epic poems of the past—poetry created under divine inspiration, revealing what humans on their own can never see or know, describing the world of gods and the world of humans and the meetings between humans and gods.

And he wrote it in three parts. The first part describes his journey to the goddess who has no name. The second describes what she taught him about reality. Then the last part starts with the goddess saying, Now I'm going to deceive you; and she goes on to describe, in detail, the world we believe we live in.

Every single figure Parmenides encounters in his poem is a woman or a girl. Even the animals are female, and he's taught by a goddess. The universe he describes is a feminine one; and if this man's poem represents the starting point for western logic, then something very strange has happened for logic to end up the way it has.

The journey he describes is mythical, a journey to the divine with the help of the divine. It's not a journey like any other journey. But because it's mythical doesn't mean it isn't real. On the contrary, anyone who makes that journey discovers the journeys we're used to making are the ones that are unreal. Perhaps you've noticed it —that our awareness is completely motionless, never changes. When we walk down the road we're really not going anywhere. We can travel around the world and we're not going anywhere at all. We never go anywhere; if we think we do we're just caught in the web of appearances, caught in the web of our senses.

For centuries people have struggled to make sense of the journey Parmenides describes. Most often they explain it as a literary device, a poetic strategy that he used to give authority to his ideas. They say the divine figures are nothing but symbols for his reasoning powers—he was, after all, a philosopher—and the journey itself is an allegory for his battle out of darkness into clarity, from ignorance to intellectual enlightenment.

But there's no need to struggle like this. It's such a strain to have to explain one thing as meaning something else, and we've tired our minds out for so long avoiding what's in front of us. Plato had good reasons for killing him over two thousand years ago; to go on killing him now is pointless.

And the fact is that Parmenides never describes himself as travelling out of darkness into the light. When you follow what he says you see he was going in exactly the opposite direction.

In the old days the best interpreters —of oracles, of the riddles of existence, of how birds sang and how they flew—knew that the greatest part of interpretation was not to interfere but simply to watch, and listen, and allow the things observed to reveal their meaning.

PARMENIDES doesn't say straightaway who the young women are who guide him on his journey. He was too fine a poet for that. Like the best of the Greek poets before him he knew how to use the technique of suspense and gradual explanation. Eventually he says who they are, but not to begin with.

They had come into the light to meet him. Now they're taking him somewhere else. They had come out of the Mansions of Night, and we know from the great Greek poets where those mansions are. They're in the depths of the depths, at the edges of existence, where earth and heaven have their roots: they're in Tartarus, where even the gods are afraid to go.

And they take him to the gates that Day and Night come out of whenever they emerge—now one, now the other—to move through the world. We know from the same Greek poets where those gates are. They're in the depths of the depths, right at the entrance to the

Mansions of Night. The girls are taking Parmenides back where they've come from.

And as the doorkeeper opens up to let them through, the gates move apart to create a huge chasm. The same Greek poets talk about the great chasm that lies just behind those gates. It's the chasm of Tartarus, by the Mansions of Night.

Parmenides writes in a way that's very simple, and very subtle. He deliberately uses images and expressions that were familiar to his listeners so he can evoke a whole setting or a scene. This is how poets wrote in his day. They wouldn't say outright what they were talking about: they wouldn't have to. They would talk in hints instead. There was no need to say 'This is Tartarus'; they would use words and expressions that the great poets had used before them and the listener would understand.

That's not to say they copied exactly what the poets before them had said. They didn't: each new generation had to discover and describe reality for itself. But the basic reference points were always stable. Make everything explicit and you tire your listeners. Speak indirectly, through hints and pointers, and you give them credit for their intelligence; this is what they wanted, what they asked for. That's how people used to speak and write in the old days. It was very subtle and very simple.

So Parmenides' journey is down to the underworld, into the regions of Hades and Tartarus from where no one usually returns. And once you start to understand this then all the other details fall into their place. He was travelling in the direction of his own death, consciously and willingly; and the only way to describe that is in the language of myth, because myth is just the world of meaning we've left behind.

The mares that carry me as far as longing can reach
rode on, once they had come and fetched me onto the legendary
road of the divinity that carries the man who knows
through the vast and dark unknown. And on I was carried
as the mares, aware just where to go, kept carrying me
straining at the chariot; and young women led the way.
And the axle in the hubs let out the sound of a pipe
blazing from the pressure of the two well-rounded wheels
at either side, as they rapidly led on: young women, girls,
daughters of the Sun who had left the mansions of Night
for the light and pushed back the veils from their faces
with their hands.
There are the gates of the pathways of Night and Day,
held fast in place between the lintel above and a threshold of stone;
and they reach up into the heavens, filled with gigantic doors.
And the keys—that now open, now lock—are held fast by
Justice: she who always demands exact returns. And with
soft seductive words the girls cunningly persuaded her to

push back immediately, just for them, the bar that bolts
the gates. And as the doors flew open, making the bronze
axles with their pegs and nails spin—now one, now the other—
in their pipes, they created a gaping chasm. Straight through and
on the girls held fast their course for the chariot and horses,
straight down the road.

And the goddess welcomed me kindly, and took
my right hand in hers and spoke these words as she addressed me:
'Welcome young man, partnered by immortal charioteers,
reaching our home with the mares that carry you. For it was
no hard fate that sent you travelling this road—so far away
from the beaten track of humans—but Rightness, and Justice.
And what's needed is for you to learn all things: both the unshaken
heart of persuasive Truth and the opinions of mortals,
in which there's nothing that can truthfully be trusted at all.
But even so, this too you will learn—how beliefs based on
appearance ought to be believable as they travel all through
all there is.'

The Man in a Toga

THE YEAR: 1958. VELIA.

There are some things nobody and nothing can take away from you. For Pellegrino Claudio Sestieri the fact that his discoveries were rushed into print by others before he was able to get a word in edgeways could never change the reality of what he had found.

And his discoveries weren't just normal ones. Black holes out there in the universe are nothing compared to the black holes in our own past. Those holes are much more than ordinary gaps. They have the power to destroy our ideas about ourselves and bring us face to face with nothingness.

You could say it all started with the man in a toga. Sestieri's team found him in a large old building with a hidden gallery down by the harbour. He was around two thousand years old—from what we'd now call the time of Christ. Only about a century later the structure of the building was altered and that's where he was discovered: buried in the new foundations. He was no longer needed for anything else.

But the sculpture itself wasn't what mattered. What was important was the inscription that can still be read on its base. And it wasn't the only inscription. Two others were found in the same place, on bases that had hardly managed to survive intact; the statues they'd once supported were gone.

The three inscriptions were the first pieces in a puzzle, a puzzle that it would take the greater part of ten years to put together. But when Sestieri's successor, Mario Napoli, finally held the last of the pieces in his hands he still didn't see the message the puzzle had been spelling out. And no one else did.

All the facts and figures and dates and details seemed somehow so significant: so important to try to explain, and above all so important to ignore. And yet they were just a trick, a façade. For behind them is a reality that has no place, no past, no time.

And once you let yourself be touched by that nothing is ever the same.

THE INSCRIPTION carved in Greek at the feet of the man in a toga seemed simple enough.

Oulis son of Euxinus citizen of Velia healer
Phôlarchos in the 379th year.

The other two inscriptions kept to the same pattern:

Oulis son of Aristôn healer Phôlarchos in the 280th year

and

Oulis son of Hieronymus healer Phôlarchos in the 446th year.

Understanding the first word is easy. We know what it means, we know its history, we know where it comes from. Oulis was the name of someone dedicated to the god Apollo—to Apollo Oulios as he was sometimes called.

Apollo Oulios had his own special areas of worship, mainly in the western coastal regions of Anatolia. And as for the title Oulios, it contains a delightful ambiguity. Originally it meant 'deadly', 'destructive', 'cruel': every god has his destructive side. But Greeks also explained it another way, as meaning 'he who makes whole'. That, in a word, is Apollo—the destroyer who heals, the healer who destroys.

If it was just a matter of a single person called Oulis you couldn't draw too many conclusions. But a string of three inscriptions all starting with the same name, this name, isn't a coincidence; and the way each of the men is referred to as Oulis makes one thing very plain. As the first people who published the texts already saw, these were men connected with Apollo not on a casual basis but systematically—from generation to generation.

We don't have to look far to see what's involved. Every person mentioned on the inscriptions is called 'healer' as well. The Greek word is Iatros. But Apollo was known as Iatros himself: it was one of his favourite titles. At Rome too, to the north, he was known as 'Apollo the healer'. And this was true above all of Apollo Oulios. If you were to look up the ancient Greek dictionaries under the entry for Oulios you'd find the explanation 'Apollo. For he was a healer.'

So as healers these men were doing what Apollo did. Apollo was their god; and they were his representatives on earth.

JUST AS ALL THREE MEN being given the same name is no coincidence, it's no accident either that Apollo Oulios had his centres of worship around the coastal regions of Anatolia. This is where the Velians came from when they left Phocaea for the west.

The worship of Apollo happens to have been famous back at Phocaea. But that's only a part of the point. There are so many signs—the coins they made, the design of their buildings, the details of their religion—that show how faithfully the Velians followed the ways of their ancestors. In his story about the Phocaeans Herodotus takes special care to describe how they made a priority of rescuing the sacred objects from their temples before they fled the Persians: to emphasize that they took their religious traditions with them when they left the coast of Asia for Italy. The case of Apollo proves how right he was.

And then there's the men's name itself, Oulis. Words carry a stamp, the mark of their own past. And they carry it wherever they go. Outside of Velia or Velia's sphere of influence the name is never heard of in the western Mediterranean—except in just one place. That place was in the region of what's now Marseilles: the other great colony founded by the Phocaeans. The pattern of the evidence tells its own story, leaves no room for doubt. The name Oulis was carried to southern France, as it was carried to southern Italy, from the mother city of Phocaea.

Those three inscriptions for the men called Oulis were carved in stone at around the time of Christ. But the details on them are much more than a fantasy in the mind of whoever carved them. The traditions they refer to reach back far into the past.

The time periods on the inscriptions—280 years, 379 years, 446 years—sound immense, and yet they correspond to reality. The three healers belonged to a tradition stretching back well over five hundred years, back to before Velia had even been founded by the Phocaeans.

As for the starting point used to calculate all the datings, it would only be a matter of time before the pieces of the puzzle made that clear. But first there were other details to make sense of, details that it's so easy to pass over. For they were the key to things we no longer know or can even imagine.

THE FIRST THING THE GODDESS DOES AFTER Parmenides arrives is reassure him: reassure him that what brought him to her 'was no hard fate'. Those words 'hard fate' have a very specific meaning in ancient Greek. They're a standard expression for death.

Her reassurance would be pointless unless there was good reason to suppose death is what had brought him to her. She's saying, without having to say it any more clearly, that you'd only expect to arrive where he has arrived if you were dead.

So that's what he has done—travelled the road of death while still alive, gone where the dead go without dying. For anyone else the place he's come to would be deadly.

There's just one passage in Greek literature that comes close to Parmenides' description of his welcome. It's a passage describing the welcome waiting for the great hero Heracles when he went down to the underworld alive: the queen of the dead greets him as warmly as she would greet her own brother. By Parmenides' time it was well understood that brute force and bravery weren't enough to take a hero down to the world of the dead. He had to know what he's doing, where he's going; know how he stands in relation to the gods. He had to have been initiated into the mysteries of the underworld.

It's the same with Parmenides. Right at the beginning of his poem he says he's a 'man who knows'. People have realized for a long time that in ancient Greek this was a standard way of referring to the initiate—to those who know what others don't and because of what they know are able to go where others won't.

And for them the welcome, there in the world of the dead, has such kindness and such warmth.

THERE ARE SO MANY OTHER HINTS in Parmenides' poem about where it is he's going. Those huge gates he comes to—they're guarded by Justice. Justice for the Greeks was a goddess, a goddess who had to be able to keep a watch on everything that's happening in the world. But when it was a question of stating where she lives, the clearest answer from the Greek poets was that 'she shares the same house as the gods of the underworld'.

This is just a part of the story. If we forget Parmenides came from southern Italy then everything goes wrong.

What he writes about is beyond time and place; but to understand it you have to start from time and place. People have been so baffled by his poem, made it out to be such a lifeless thing, baffled everyone else. That's only because they refuse to see it against its background—in terms of the traditions he inherited and the place he came from. Cut something off from its roots and of course it's got no life.

Vase after vase has been found in southern Italy painted with pictures of the underworld. Justice is there, together with the queen of the dead and the hero who's able to reach her.

Sometimes the hero is Orpheus—Orpheus the magician who managed to make the journey through the power of his songs. In Italy Orpheus wasn't just some sentimental figure from myth. He was much more. He was the focus for mystical and poetic traditions about the underworld, and Velia itself was a centre for those traditions. One of the oldest Orphic poems described how Justice lives together with the other powers of cosmic law at the entrance to a vast cave: the cave that's the home of Night.

Then there's the way the goddess greets Parmenides. She welcomes him 'kindly'—the word means 'favourably', 'kindly', 'warmly'—and gives him her right hand. Nothing was more important than finding a kind and favourable welcome when you went down to the world of the dead.

The alternative was annihilation. And there in the underworld the right hand signals acceptance, favour. The left hand means destruction. That's why Orphic texts were written on gold and buried with initiates in southern Italy, to remind them how to keep to the right and how to make sure the queen of the dead receives them 'kindly'. The word on the texts and the word Parmenides uses— they're one and the same.

And for these people, just as in the case of Heracles, it was all a matter of finding their own link with the divine. That's what initiation was: to find out how you're related to the world of the divine, know how you belong, how you're at home there just as much as here. It was to become adopted, a child of the gods. For those people it was all a matter of being prepared before you die, making the connection between this world and that. Otherwise it's too late.

IT'S SUCH A PERFECT ARRANGEMENT for wisdom to hide away in death. Everyone runs from death so everyone runs away from wisdom, except for those who are willing to pay the price and go against the stream.

Parmenides' journey takes him in exactly the opposite direction from everything we value, out of life as we know it and straight towards what we fear most of all. It takes him far from ordinary experience, from 'the beaten track of humans'.

There are no people here, nothing familiar at all, no towns, no cities—however hard that is to accept, however easy it is to want to slip what we already know into the things he says. For what he's describing are regions that to us are completely unknown.

Later on in his poem he explains that night and darkness are the equivalent of ignorance. This can seem amazing: that he should go to the depths of ignorance in search of wisdom instead of straight to the light. But, in Greek, words that mean 'unknowing' also mean 'unknown'; it's the same with 'ignorant' and 'ignored'. Ignorance for Parmenides is only what's ignorance in terms of ordinary human experience, with all its narrowness and limitations. It's ignorance simply because it's ignored, ignored by people who run from death. And what everyone ignores—that's where wisdom lies.

To die before you die, no longer to live on the surface of yourself: this is what Parmenides is pointing to. It demands tremendous courage. The journey he describes changes your body; it alters every cell. Mythologically it's the journey of the hero, the great heroes like Heracles or Orpheus. And yet to understand what's involved we have to forget all our concepts of what it means to be a hero. In the Italy of Parmenides' time the idea of what a hero is was far more profound.

Already at the start of his poem Parmenides mentions the essential thing for making the journey—the longing, the passion or desire. He's taken to where he goes, but he's only taken 'as far as longing can reach'. We usually think of a hero as a warrior, a fighter. And yet what gets Parmenides where he goes isn't willpower; it isn't struggle or effort. He doesn't have to do anything. He's just taken, taken straight where he needs to go. And the longing isn't what gets him there, either: the strength of his longing simply determines how far he can go. It seems such a straightforward statement, but it's one of the hardest things to understand.

Our own longing hardly adds up to anything. It's enough to take us lunging from one desire to another; that's all. We scatter it everywhere in wanting this or that: satisfy our desires and never satisfy ourselves. And we never can be satisfied. Our longing is so deep, so immense that nothing in this world of appearances can ever hold it or contain it. So we break it up instead, keep throwing it away—want this, then that, until we're old and exhausted.

It seems easy; everyone does it. But it's so hard to have to keep running from the hollowness we all feel inside, such a heroic task to have to keep finding substitutes to fill the void.

The other way's so easy, but it seems so hard. It's just a matter of knowing how to turn and face our own longing without interfering with it or doing anything at all. And that goes against the grain of everything we're used to, because we've been taught in so many ways to escape from ourselves—find a thousand good reasons for avoiding our longing.

Sometimes it appears as depression, calling us away from everything we think we want, pulling us into the darkness of ourselves. The voice is so familiar that we run from it in every way we can; the more powerful the call the further we run. It has the power to make us mad, and yet it's so innocent: the voice of ourselves calling to ourselves. The strange thing is that the negativity isn't in the depression—it's in running from the depression. And what we're afraid of really isn't what we're afraid of at all.

Always we want to learn from outside, from absorbing other people's knowledge. It's safer that way. The trouble is that it's always other people's knowledge. We already have everything we need to know, in the darkness inside ourselves. The longing is what turns us inside out until we find the sun and the moon and stars inside.

THOSE GIRLS who guide Parmenides on his journey to the underworld, they're daughters of the Sun.

That sounds strange, quite a paradox. For us the sun is up above in the light, doesn't have anything to do with darkness or death. But this isn't because we're any wiser or because we've managed to leave the world of myth behind: that would be about as easy as leaving our own death behind. The reason why to us it sounds strange is because we've lost any contact with the underworld.

The underworld isn't just a place of darkness and death. It only seems like that from a distance. In reality it's the supreme place of paradox where all the opposites meet. Right at the roots of western as well as eastern mythology there's the idea that the sun comes out of the underworld and goes back to the underworld every night. It belongs in the underworld. That's where it has its home; where its children come from. The source of light is at home in the darkness.

This was well understood in southern Italy. A whole Italian mythology grew up around the figure of the sun god as he's driven in his chariot by the horses that carry him out of the underworld before they take him down again. That was true at Velia too. And for certain men and women known as Pythagoreans—people who had gathered around Pythagoras when he came out to southern Italy from the east—the same ideas were a basic tradition. Those people were familiar with Orphic traditions; used them. Heracles was their hero.

Pythagoreans tended to live close to volcanic regions. For them that was something very meaningful. They saw volcanic fire as the light in the depths of darkness: it was the fire of hell, but also the fire that all the light we know and see derives from. For them the light of the sun and moon and stars were just reflections, offshoots of the invisible fire inside the underworld. And they understood that there's no going up without going down, no heaven without going through hell. To them the fire in the underworld was purifying, transforming, immortalizing. Everything was part of a process and there were no short cuts. Everything had to be experienced, included; and to find clarity meant facing utter darkness.

This is much more than just a matter of mythology. In theory we think we know that each dawn brings a new day, but in practice we never see what that means. Deep down we've all agreed to look for light in the light and avoid everything else: reject the darkness, the depths. Those people realized there's something very important hidden in the depths. For them it wasn't only a question of confronting a little bit of darkness inside themselves— of dipping their feet in their feelings, paddling in the pond of their emotions and trying to bring them into the light of day. It was a question of going right through the darkness to what lies at the other end.

That's not a pleasant challenge to live with. Our minds are defeated even by the prospect. So when Plato and his followers took over these ideas from the Pythagoreans they cleverly amputated the ambiguities: focused only on the true and the good and the beautiful, and cut out the need for the descent. We no longer even notice what happened.

Then there were early Christians who talked about the 'depths' of the divine. Most of them were soon silenced. And there were Jewish mystics who spoke of 'descending' to the divine; they were silenced too. It's far simpler to keep the divine somewhere up above, at a safe distance. The trouble is that when the divine is removed from the depths we lose our depth, start viewing the depths with fear and end up struggling, running from ourselves, trying to lift ourselves up by our bootstraps into the beyond.

It's impossible to reach the light at the cost of rejecting darkness. The darkness haunts us; we're chased by our own depths. But the knowledge of the other way was left only for a few heretics, and writers of oracles, and for the alchemists.

In that knowledge there's no dogma. It's too subtle for that. It's not even a matter of attitude but simply a question of perception—the perception that light belongs in darkness, clarity in obscurity, that darkness can't be rejected for the sake of light because everything contains its opposite.

That's why Parmenides' journey takes him precisely to the point where all the opposites meet: the point where Day and Night both come out from, the mythical place where earth and heaven have their source. And that's why he describes the gates he comes to as having their threshold in Tartarus but 'reaching up into the heavens'. They're where the upper and the lower meet, at exactly the same point where earlier poets had described Atlas standing with his feet in the lower world but holding up the heavens with his head and hands.

This is the place that gives access to the depths and also to the world above. You can go up and you can go down. It's a point on the axis of the universe: the axis that joins what's above and what's below. But first you have to descend to this point before you're able to ascend, die before you can be reborn. To reach there, where every direction is available and everything merges with its opposite, you have to go down into the darkness—into the world of death where Night and Day both come from.

As soon as she's welcomed him, the first thing the goddess does is call Parmenides 'young man'. That's just one word in Greek: *kouros*. A *kouros* is a young man, a boy, a son or child.

There are experts who say this is Parmenides' way of presenting himself as someone under thirty years old. Others say it's the goddess' way of confronting him with his lack of wisdom and experience. The truth is far more subtle.

Kouros is an ancient word, older even than the Greek language. Often it's a title of honour, never an expression of contempt. When the great poets before Parmenides

71

used the term it was always to communicate a sense of nobility. It was the *kouros*, more than anyone else, who was a hero.

In terms of physical age it could mean someone under thirty. But in practice the word had a far wider meaning. A *kouros* was the man of any age who still saw life as a challenge, who faced it with the whole of his vigour and passion, who hadn't yet stood back to make way for his sons. The word indicated the quality of a man, not how old he was.

It was also closely connected with initiation. The *kouros* stands at the borderline between the world of the human and the world of the divine; has access to them both, is loved and recognized in both. It's only as a *kouros* that the initiate can possibly succeed at the great ordeal of making a journey into the beyond—just as Parmenides does.

The *kouros* has a great deal in common with the world of the divine. In their own way they're both time-less, untouched by age. When Heracles dies and is made immortal, it's as a *kouros* that he's pictured rising up from the funeral pyre. And the situation of the nameless *kouros* face to face with the nameless goddess, just like Parmenides—this was a well-known scenario in the mysteries of initiation.

A *kouros* was often essential for gaining access to the world of the gods. He was needed for prophecy, for receiving oracles, for the magical process of lying down in a special place at night to obtain messages from the gods through dreams. He was needed because of his sensitivity, his ability to distance himself from the usual human thoughts; because he wouldn't try to interfere unconsciously or consciously with what he heard and received. It was possible for an older person to perform the role of the *kouros*, but then he had to have the innocence and purity of a child.

Contact with what's timeless doesn't leave you as you are, even though outwardly it can seem to. It takes away your past. That's why the initiate has his old life taken away, is given a 'second destiny' instead—is born again, adopted by the gods. And the tough hero becomes a little child.

Italian sculptures and paintings tell it all: the great hero Heracles as a bearded man reduced to the role of an infant, initiates with the bodies of new-born babies but the faces of old men and women.

The hero doesn't just hold in his hand the mythical map for the colonizer to follow. He also holds the map for the initiate, and it's the map of immortality. This going back to the state of a child doesn't have anything to do with physical age. And it has nothing to do with immaturity, either. It isn't some state of naivety to grow out of or go beyond.

On the contrary, this is the only real maturity there is: the maturity of struggling beyond the physical world and discovering that you're also at home somewhere else.

As for immaturity, that's when we grow old and empty because we've missed the opportunities life always brings for making conscious contact with the timeless.

❀

THE WORLD OF THE DIVINE for Greeks was the world of the *kourotrophos*, 'nurturer of the *kouros*'. This was a common title for their goddesses and gods.

The *kourotrophos* cares for young men and young women, sustains and guides them in a way no human parent possibly can. But the relationship is completely different from ordinary human relationships of dependence: it's something far more paradoxical. For the world of the gods doesn't only contain the nourishment that young men or women need. It also contains the most essential aspect of themselves.

The *kouros* isn't just a human figure. That's only one side of him. He's a god as well, the exact image of the human *kouros* in the world of the divine; and the most important god of all for a human *kouros* was Apollo. Apollo was the divine *kouros* and the god of the *kouros*. He was his model, his immortal image and embodiment.

And there, in the world of the gods, the human *kouros* also has his female counterparts: divine *kourai*, immortal young women or girls. They're young like him, except that as goddesses they play the role of *kourotrophos* too—the role of protector and guide for the hero.

The first thing Parmenides is told when he arrives in the underworld is 'Welcome young man, partnered by immortal charioteers.' But people don't care too much what he's told, so they translate it as 'Welcome young man, accompanied by immortal charioteers.'

That sounds a much simpler statement for the goddess to make. And yet it's also to misunderstand the meaning of a word that in Greek always has the sense of partnership—of inseparability, intimacy, of an enduring bond that sustains and never ends. In human terms it can be the bond between brothers and sisters, but above all the intimacy of the partnership between a husband and wife.

So Parmenides is saying how he's bound to the charioteers who brought him to the underworld, the charioteers that right from the beginning he refers to as *kourai*—young women, girls, daughters of the Sun.

He arrives as a *kouros* together with *kourai*, and it couldn't be otherwise. The place he's reached is a place where everything comes together with its opposite: earth and heaven, night and day, light and darkness but also male and female, mortality and immortality, death and youthfulness. And even the fact that his partners are daughters of the Sun, beings of light who are at home in the darkness, couldn't be more appropriate. Later Parmenides explains how—in terms of the grand illusion we live in—humans themselves are originally solar beings, children of the sun.

Death for us seems just nothingness, where we have to leave everything behind. But it's also a fullness that can hardly be conceived of, where everything is in contact with everything and nothing is ever lost. And yet to know that, you have to be able to become conscious in the world of the dead.

Masters of Dreams

O FTEN WORDS ARE ONLY WORDS. SOMETIMES they're not: sometimes they have the power to open up a whole world—to give reality to things that have always been hovering on the horizon of our consciousness, just out of reach.

All three of the Greek inscriptions discovered at Velia by Sestieri mention a word that hasn't been found anywhere else in the world. It had only ever been encountered once before. A curious Italian advocate had come across it one day inscribed, in its Latin form, on a piece of stone at Velia; he published it as a little amusement in 1832. And it wasn't long after Sestieri's three discoveries there that the faded remains of another Latin inscription, also containing the same word, were found carved on a large fragment of marble. The text was so fragmentary, and so faded, that it was about the only word you could read any more.

Otherwise it's unheard of in the whole of Greek and Latin literature. It's Phôlarchos.

The word may well be unique, unknown outside of Velia. And yet that's not to say it can't be understood. But scholars are strange creatures. When they're faced with some new evidence they like to add one and one together and arrive at one and a half; then they spend years arguing about what happened to the other half. The half that's missing is the ability to watch and listen—to follow the evidence where it leads, however unfamiliar.

Phôlarchos is a combination of two words: *phôleos* and *archos*. *Archos* means a lord, a chief, the person in charge. But it's the first half that's unusual.

A *phôleos* is a lair where animals hide, a den. Often it's a cave. Any other senses of the word derived from this. Ancient Greek dictionaries say it could sometimes be used, just as you'd expect, to describe 'dens' of human activity. But that's little more than street slang: nothing of any relevance to the titles on the carved inscriptions.

They also say it could be used as a name for special places in a house or temple, places where religious groups came together. That sounds much more to the point; but it's not enough. The trouble is that those dictionaries were put together at a time when the language was almost dying out. Often the people who wrote them were just guessing, groping in the dark. There are no real answers here—only pointers on the way.

❀

IN THE WHOLE HISTORY of the Greek language, through from the earliest times to how it's spoken nowadays, *phôleos* always has the same basic meaning. It's a place where animals go into retreat: where they lie motionless, absolutely still, hardly breathing. They sleep there, or they stay in a state similar to sleep, or they hibernate.

That's why expressions like 'being in a lair' or 'lying in a lair'—*phôleia* and *phôleuein* were the words in ancient Greek—came to mean being in a state of suspended animation. They could be used to describe a woman from southern Anatolia who would go into a state of hibernation for months at a time. The only way you could tell she was alive was from her breathing. And early doctors would use the words to describe the state of apparent death, of suspended animation when the pulse is so quiet you can hardly feel it.

So the men called Phôlarchos on those inscriptions from Velia—they were in charge of a lair, a place of suspended animation. That doesn't make much sense. It doesn't even sound worth making sense of; but it is. And we don't have to look far to see what it means. The answer is in the inscriptions themselves.

Those people called Phôlarchos were healers, and healing in the ancient world had a great deal to do with states of suspended animation. It was all tied up in a clumsy-sounding word: incubation.

To incubate is just to lie down in a place. But the word had a very particular meaning. Before the beginnings of what's known as 'rational' medicine in the West, healing always had to do with the divine. If people were sick it was normal to go to the shrines of gods, or else to the shrines of great beings who once had been humans but now were more than humans: the heroes. And they'd lie down.

They would lie down in an enclosed space. Often it was a cave. And either they'd fall asleep and have a dream or they'd enter a state described as neither sleep nor waking—and eventually they'd have a vision. Sometimes the vision or the dream would bring them face to face with the god or the goddess or hero, and that was how the healing came about. People were healed like this all the time.

What's important is that you would do absolutely nothing. The point came when you wouldn't struggle or make an effort. You'd just have to surrender to your condition. You would lie down as if you were dead; wait without eating or moving, sometimes for days at a time. And you'd wait for the healing to come from somewhere else, from another level of awareness and another level of being.

But that's not to say you were left alone. There would be people in charge of the place—priests who understood how the process worked and how to supervise it, who knew how to help you understand what you needed to know without interfering with the process itself.

We still have priests, except that now they belong to a different religion. Underneath the surface of the rhetoric and persuasion there's not much to choose between modern science and ancient magic. But because there's no knowledge left any more of how to find access to what's beyond our waking consciousness we have to take anaesthetics and drugs. And because there's no longer any understanding of powers greater than ourselves we're denied any meaning to our suffering. So we suffer as liabilities, die as statistics.

THE SIMILARITIES between lying down like an animal in a lair and lying down for incubation in a shrine are obvious enough. But there's no need to guess that the Greeks were aware of the similarities. We know they were.

Two thousand years ago a man called Strabo wrote a passage describing the countryside of western Anatolia. He was talking about an area to the south of Phocaea, in a region called Caria. It was an area he knew well. This is where he once lived and studied.

And in the passage he describes a famous cave there, known as a Charonium or entrance to the underworld. Next to it was a temple dedicated to the gods of the underworld: to Pluto—one of the titles given to Hades—and his wife Persephone, who was often referred to as 'the Maiden'. It was usual Greek practice not to mention the divinities of the underworld by name.

On the road leading from Tralles to Nysa there's a village that belongs to the people of Nysa. And there, not far from the city of Acharaca, that's where the Plutonium is—the entrance to the underworld. There's a sacred precinct there, very well-endowed, and a temple to Pluto and the Maiden. And the Charonium is a cave just above the precinct. The place is quite amazing. For what they say is that people who fall ill and are willing to submit to the methods of healing offered by these two divinities come here and live for a while in the village together with the most experienced among the priests. And these priests lie down and sleep in the cave on behalf of the sick, then they prescribe treatments on the basis of the dreams they receive. It's these same men who also invoke the healing power of the gods.

But often they lead the sick into the cave instead and settle them down, then leave them there in utter stillness (*hêsychia*) without any food for several days—just like animals in a lair (*phôleos*). And sometimes those who are afflicted by illness have dreams of their own, dreams that they take very seriously. And yet even then they still rely on the others, as priests, to perform the role of guides and advisors by introducing them to the mysteries. For anyone else the place is forbidden territory, and deadly.

Every detail in the account has its significance. But it's enough just to notice the incubation in a cave, the dreams, the state of utter stillness—and the fact that at this cave in Caria the sick are described as lying for days on end 'like animals in a lair'.

And there are the priests to guide them through the process, often keeping to the background but always firmly in charge: the masters of dreams, lords of the lair.

AT VELIA those men called Phôlarchos were related to Apollo. Here, at the cave alongside the road in Caria, there's no mention of Apollo. But he's not far away.

If thousands of years ago you followed the road further inland you came to a town called Hierapolis— and to another Plutonium, another entrance to the underworld. There the religious practices were almost identical to the ones at the Plutonium described by Strabo. And there at Hierapolis, right above the cave, was a temple to Apollo: an Anatolian Apollo, god of the sun.

This is perfectly understandable. For Apollo wasn't just a god of healing. He was also a god of incubation. At Hierapolis itself, people slept in the sanctuary during the night for the sake of having dreams. And at the greatest incubation centres in Italy or Greece or Anatolia, Apollo was always there. If he wasn't the chief god, he was somewhere in the background.

Often those centres were shrines of Asclepius, or they were shrines of heroes. The heroes were usually considered children of Apollo—and so was Asclepius. He owed his knowledge of healing to his father, and most of his incubation centres had once been centres for the worship of Apollo. Even after Asclepius became the most famous Greek god of incubation he still shared his own shrines, as well as the honours people gave him, with Apollo.

And that's more or less how things remained right through to the end of the ancient world. When magicians in the centuries after Christ wanted to experience revelations or receive knowledge through dreams, Apollo was the god they invoked through incubation in the darkness of the night.

Lairs and incubation, Apollo and incubation—nearly all the links are there to explain why those healers in Velia, priests of Apollo, were called lords of a lair. Nearly all, but not quite.

ISTRIA: an ancient Greek colony on the shores of the Black Sea, at the mouth of the Danube. Now it would be near the Romanian–Ukrainian frontier. That sounds a long way from Velia; but history has its own patterns of flow and interaction.

The Black Sea was well known to the Phocaeans. They created colonies there themselves hand in hand with the leading colonizers of the region—the people of Miletus. Miletus was the most famous Greek city in ancient Caria, and Istria was founded from there.

One of the greatest centres for the worship of Apollo Oulios was at Miletus. The Phocaeans knew a great deal about how people from Miletus worshipped Apollo: one of the colonies on the Black Sea that the two cities both helped to found came to be called Apollonia in his honour. And it was because of his importance at Miletus that Apollo the healer was worshipped in Istria too.

There at Istria a family of priests was dedicated to serving Apollo the healer, from generation to generation. And there, in the sacred temple area, two words were found inscribed on a slab of marble. The words were Apollo Phôleutêrios.

Archaeologists have worried about what the title Phôleutêrios could mean. The man who discovered the inscription simply said 'I confess I don't begin to understand.' Others have been more persevering: have tried to give it the meaning 'Apollo who hides away' in the sense of 'Apollo who protects from evil'. But that's impossible; Greeks wouldn't express the idea this way. There's only one thing it can mean. It means 'Apollo who hides away in a lair'—his title as the incubator god, the god of suspended animation.

Apollo the healer as Phôleutêrios in Istria, priests of Apollo the healer as Phôlarchos at Velia: the two titles are obviously related, offshoots of the same tradition. Apollo was the god of whoever lies down like an animal in a lair. And as his human representatives, the healers from Velia were Lords of the Lair.

These were old ideas, ancient practices—practices that had their home in western Asia and especially in Caria. For the Anatolian origin of the name Phôlarchos is proved by Istria just as the Anatolian origin of the name Oulis is proved by Marseilles. Both words belonged to the traditions that the Phocaeans took out with them to Italy when they left the coast of Asia for the West.

The pieces were starting to fall into place.

Apollo

THESE TRADITIONS LINKING APOLLO WITH incubation and caves and dark places: they have nothing at all to do with the Apollo we've become used to.

Nowadays he's considered the divine embodiment of reason and rationality—as if a god could ever be reasonable in the sense that we attribute to the word. The history of how this notion came to be substituted for an awareness of the things he used to be is an absurd one, the way such stories usually are. It reaches back a long time, and the story hasn't yet finished. Attempts have been made at rationalizing Asclepius but they never lasted long. The rationalizing of Apollo still goes on.

Normally he's described as the most Greek of all the gods: a perfect image of the ancient Greek spirit, all clarity and brightness.

But he wasn't clear at all. Above anything else he was a god of oracles and prophecy—and the oracles he gave out were riddles, full of ambiguities and traps. It was the people who believed everything was bright and clear who ended up in trouble.

Often he's associated with bright music and song. And yet, especially in Anatolia, he had a very different side. There songs were sung in his honour that were full of strange words, sung in an incantatory language no one could understand. And his oracles were spoken by his prophet in a voice heavy with trance: oracles full of repetitions and riddles, expressed in a poetry that at times hardly seemed poetry at all. For Apollo was a god who operated on another level of consciousness with rules and a logic of its own.

Sometimes it's said that when magicians during the centuries after Christ invoked Apollo through incubation in the middle of the night, this was a proof of how his brightness had already faded away—along with the famous brightness of the classical world.

But the fact is that he was always associated with darkness and night. At Rome, where Greek colonists introduced the worship of Apollo the healer, the best time for incubation at his temple was in the middle of the night. And back in Anatolia there were ancient temple traditions that involved locking Apollo's priestess up with her god in the evening. When she came out the next morning she was able to prophesy because of her mystical union with him during the night.

And right from the beginning he was connected not only with night but with caves and dark places, with the underworld and death. This is why, at the Anatolian town of Hierapolis, Apollo's temple was right above the cave leading down to the underworld. And it's why at other famous oracle centres in Anatolia his temples were built just the same way—above a cave giving access to the underworld that was entered by his priest and by initiates at the dead of night.

When people started trying to make Apollo reasonable, philosophically acceptable, they were simply looking at the surface and avoiding what's underneath.

IT WAS ALSO in Anatolia that Apollo came to be associated closely with the sun.

Really his links with the sun go back far into the past. But formal statements from Greeks identifying the sun with Apollo only start appearing at a certain time, which was also the time when Parmenides was alive. And what's important about these statements is the way they indicate that the identification was esoteric—a matter for initiates only, for people familiar with 'the silent names of the gods'.

Now it's so easy to assume that Apollo and the sun are all a matter of brightness and light. But that's to forget where the sun is most at home: in the darkness of the underworld. And it's also to miss what those statements about the sun and Apollo actually say.

One of them happens to be the oldest mention in ancient literature of Orpheus' descent to the underworld. It explains how Orpheus came to be so devoted to Apollo. Tradition made him a priest and prophet of Apollo, sometimes even made him his son. But this account says it was only after he went down to the world of the dead and 'because he saw the things to be seen there just as they are' that he understood why the sun is the greatest of the gods—and is identical to Apollo. The account goes on to say how he used to wake up at night and climb a mountain so he could catch a glimpse of his god at dawn.

There was also a famous Orphic poem. It had been written by a Pythagorean in southern Italy, but hardly any traces of it have been allowed to survive. It presented Orpheus making his journey to the underworld at the site of a dream oracle, next to a volcanic crater. In other words he made his descent in another state of consciousness, in a kind of dream, using the technique of incubation.

The poem described him as making one major discovery that he brought back to the world of the living. This was the fact that Apollo shares his oracular powers with Night.

We know less about the poem than about the response it evoked from religious authorities centuries later. Orpheus was mocked for his imaginary wisdom, attacked for spreading his 'false notions' through the world. And there was a famous writer called Plutarch—

he was a good man, a good Platonist, with good sources of information about the ideas generally accepted at Delphi in his time—who put the official position clearly on record. 'Apollo and Night have nothing in common.'

And for most people they didn't any more. Experience of another world through incubation holds little value once you start to place all your trust in the apparent powers of reason.

THE MOST MYTHICAL STATEMENT OF ALL about Apollo's connections with the underworld is also the simplest one. And it's no coincidence that this, too, belongs to the traditions surrounding the figure of Orpheus—the same Orpheus who used Apollo's magic incantations to make his way down to the queen of the dead.

According to an Orphic poem Apollo and Persephone went to bed together, made love. The tradition makes perfect sense in every possible way. For something that's hardly ever noticed is how the healing powers of Apollo and his son Asclepius brought them into an intimate relationship with death. To heal is to know the limits of healing and also what lies beyond. Ultimately there's no real healing without the ability to face death itself.

Apollo is a god of healing but he's also deadly. The queen of the dead is the embodiment of death; and yet it was said that the touch of her hand is healing. As their own opposites they exchanged roles with each other—and with themselves.

This explains why, in Caria, either of them could equally well be the gods at incubation centres where people came to lie down in utter stillness like animals in a lair. The stillness is the stillness of death, but that's how the healing comes.

And it explains as well why a strange pattern keeps repeating itself in the descriptions of hero-figures who were associated with Apollo. Priests and servants of Apollo themselves, they also had the closest links with the cult and worship of Persephone.

Goddess

H E DOESN'T SAY WHO SHE IS.

Right at the beginning of his poem he describes how he's taken on the 'road of the divinity', and when you read the original Greek there's just a hint that the divinity is feminine—just the slightest suggestion, that's all. It would be hard even to start to explain how he used the ambiguity of language to say and not say at the same time. But that's the way Parmenides worked.

And when at last he meets her he simply calls her 'goddess'. People have offered the strangest of reasons why, given all sorts of explanations for who she is. There are some who claim he didn't give her a name because really she's not a goddess at all, just a philosophical abstraction. Others say she must be Justice; that she's Day or Night.

But she's none of those. Justice is her doorkeeper, and when later in the poem she comes to talk about Night and Day she says they're two illusory opposites in a world of deception. That's no way to talk about yourself.

It's such an old situation: one that's repeated time and time again in approaching the history of ourselves.

The answers to the questions we ask stare us in the face but we prefer to look somewhere else—anywhere else.

Parmenides has come down to the underworld, to the goddess who lives in the realms of the dead. The Greeks called her Persephone.

He arrives at her home just beyond the gates of Night and Day, by the chasm of Tartarus and the Mansions of Night. The great Greek poets knew very well the name of the goddess who has her home in the underworld. Just past the gates used by Night and Day, next to the chasm of Tartarus and the Mansions of Night, is the home of Hades and his wife: Persephone.

The goddess who welcomes Heracles so warmly when he goes down as an initiate to the underworld is Persephone. And in paintings of her, made during Parmenides' own lifetime, you can still see exactly how she greets him. She welcomes Heracles into her home by reaching out and giving him her right hand.

When Orpheus uses Apollo's incantations to charm his way down to the world of the dead, it's her he meets. On those vases from southern Italy that show the queen of the dead greeting him while the figure of Justice stands in the background, it's Persephone who greets him. And in the Orphic texts that were written on gold for initiates, the goddess who's expected to receive them 'kindly'— just as Parmenides' goddess receives him 'kindly'—is Persephone.

THE WAY THAT PARMENIDES doesn't name his goddess could seem like an obstacle to understanding who she is. And yet it's not.

There were good reasons for not mentioning gods or goddesses by name. At Athens 'the goddess' was Athena. Everybody knew who she was. It was perfectly clear from the context: no ambiguity, no risk of confusion.

But that's just a small aspect of the matter. For the Greeks, and not only for the Greeks, a name was power. The name of a god is the power of the god. You don't invoke a divinity in vain. And there's also the sense of divine power as a vastness—or a closeness—that's beyond the limitation of any conceivable name.

This was true above all of the gods of the underworld. People didn't talk about them a great deal. Their nature is a mystery.

It's a strange thing. Because they're there the more you speak about them here the less you say. They belong to another dimension, not this, and what's silence here is language there. Here their speech is just an oracle or riddle, and here their smile can seem like sadness.

It's possible to enter that dimension, go through death while still alive. But afterwards you don't talk very much. What you've seen is shrouded in silence. There are things that just can't be said. And when you do talk there's something different to your words because death is the place where all words come from—like sparks that have their origin in fire. Then what's said has a certain power, but not because the words mean something outside them or point somewhere else. They have power because they contain their significance and meaning inside them.

More than in the case of any other divinities it was normal not to give a name to the gods or goddesses of the underworld. Then the silence was deliberate. Any risk of confusion was accepted as a part of the mystery; ambiguity was inevitable. Things were left unclear in the same way that Parmenides doesn't leave anything too clear about the identity of his goddess.

And all across the Greek world there was one particular divinity who was constantly left unnamed—but especially through southern Italy and the regions surrounding Velia. In ordinary language, in poetry, in the statements given by oracles, it was normal simply to refer to the queen of the dead as 'goddess'.

Even when there were other important goddesses worshipped in the same city and there were plenty of opportunities for confusion, Persephone would still just be called 'the goddess'. That was enough.

So it's not only clear from the details of Parmenides' journey who his goddess is: it's even clear from his unclarity.

SHE WAS an important divinity at Velia.

Centres for the worship of Persephone weren't necessarily obvious. They weren't always the type of thing you shouted about from the rooftops; there were other divinities to look after the daily activities of towns and cities, their political and outer existence.

Mainly the worship of Persephone was in the hands of women, and women hardly wrote at all. Sometimes temples built for her and her mother Demeter aren't mentioned in one single document or report from the ancient world. Nobody knows about their existence until their remains happen to be found somewhere, inside or on the edge of famous towns.

Well over two hundred years ago, back in the eighteenth century, a local baron from southern Italy came across an old inscription on a patch of land that turned out to be the area of ancient Velia. He took it back home: 'che tengo in mia casa', I have it in my house. The inscription was written in Latin, with Greek words scattered through it. It described a formal dedication from the people of the city to Persephone.

In the nineteenth century the great scholars of western Europe couldn't find the inscription any more. To them, the Greek words mixed up with the Latin were proof that it was a forgery so they dismissed the baron as a fool or a liar. He wasn't either.

Over time the language the Velians used to speak had changed from Greek to Latin; but even so they still kept using Greek words in their Latin inscriptions. By modern standards they were extremely conservative people, like so many Italian settlements of Greeks. They held fast to their old words and traditions.

Other signs of Persephone's importance at Velia also started to emerge. A block of stone was found engraved with a dedication to her: just her name and her husband's name carved in Greek on the rock. And an area sacred to the worship she shared with her mother, Demeter, had been unearthed in a field half-way between Velia and Posidonia—a town steeped in the worship of Persephone, the same Posidonia where the stranger came from who once told the Phocaeans how to make sense of Apollo's oracle.

And then there's the evidence that's been known for centuries: the evidence from Rome. Two thousand years ago Roman writers described the great temple there that had been built for Demeter and Persephone long before them—at a time when Parmenides will still have been a young man. They pointed with pride to the fact that the temple was designed on Greek models. And they explained how right from the start it had been maintained by Greek priestesses of the goddesses who were specially trained and sent northwards to Rome, generation after generation, from Velia.

It's the same story as with the inscriptions for the Oulis healers, those priests of Apollo: later evidence pointing back to earlier traditions with five hundred years in between. The temple had been built at the beginning of the fifth century BC, when growing Roman society was extremely open to the religious traditions of Greek travellers and neighbours. But it was open to one group of Greeks in particular, people the Romans were happy to be able to deal with—the explorers and colonists from Phocaea. The people of Phocaea, then Velia and Marseilles, were very powerful at a time when Rome was still very young.

Those Roman writers were quite correct. When you look at the evidence from Rome, from Velia, also from Phocaea, it doesn't just show that the worship of Persephone and Demeter was taken up to Rome in the early days of Velia's existence. It also shows that this was the same worship the Phocaeans had once practised in Anatolia and then carried with them when they sailed out to the west.

ITALY WAS A FINE SOIL for Persephone. The land was fertile with ancient goddesses; and centuries later it was

Persephone who would provide most of the imagery and inspiration for the Catholics' Virgin Mary.

As for the Phocaeans, they were like all the other colonists who came out to Italy before or after them in that they allowed the old and the familiar to blend with the new. But there are some things that don't change. And what draws us is what somehow was already known to us at the beginning.

Iatromantis

T O GO DOWN TO THE UNDERWORLD WHEN you're dead is one thing. To go there while you're alive, prepared and knowingly, and then learn from the experience—that's another thing entirely.

In describing his journey Parmenides is referring to something very specific. If we want to understand him we need to see what.

It's all tied up with that clumsy word: incubation.

The formal side to incubation was simple enough. Usually you'd lie down in a special place where you wouldn't be disturbed. Sometimes it was a room inside a house or temple; often it was a cave or other place considered a point of entry to the underworld.

And people didn't do this just when they were sick. There used to be experts at incubation—masters at the art of going into another state of consciousness or allowing themselves to go if they were drawn there. Sometimes they did this for the sake of healing others, but the main point of incubation really wasn't the healing at all. That's simply how it seemed. What was most important was the fact that the healing comes from another level of being, from somewhere else. For these were people who were able to enter another world, make contact with the divine, receive knowledge directly from the gods.

There was a man from Crete: in the Cretan dialect he was known as a *kouros*. Legends about him described how he slept for years in a sacred cave and learned everything he knew through a dream. It was said that for him dreams were his teachers—that really he had no human teacher because his teacher was his dream.

Afterwards he became famous for his ability to heal whole cities; and the traditions about him made it quite clear where his powers of healing came from. They came from what he discovered about the world of the dead and the judgement of the dead, from 'his encounters while dreaming with gods and the teachings of gods and with Justice and Truth'. It's not difficult to see the links within links and patterns within patterns: to be reminded of Parmenides' descent to the world of the dead, of his encounters with gods and the teachings of gods, of the way he keeps referring in his poem to the divine figures of Justice and Truth.

Then there was Pythagoras. When he left his home island of Samos for Italy he took Anatolian traditions with him—techniques of incubation, techniques for descending to the world of the dead. As a sign of how dedicated he was to the goddesses of the underworld he made his new home in southern Italy into a temple: built a special underground room where he'd go and stay motionless for long periods of time. Afterwards he'd describe how he had gone down to the underworld and come back as a messenger from the gods.

The reports about him say he taught his closest disciples to do the same thing, and the language of the reports shows it was the practice of incubation that he taught them. The mysteries of the underworld remained central for later Pythagoreanism—and so did the role that Pythagoreans kept giving to incubation. For this wasn't a tradition of people who were fond of ideas and beautiful theories. They were people who knew how to die before they died.

THE SIMILARITIES between lying down for incubation and approaching the state of death were very clear to the Greeks. They were obvious enough from the deathlike stillness, from the way that incubation sites were seen as points of entry to the underworld.

But there's one piece of evidence that points more directly than anything else to the links between incubation and the world of the dead.

We've already come across it. It's the passage by the writer called Strabo that describes the temple in Caria dedicated to the god of the underworld and his wife, to Persephone and Hades—that describes how people allowed into the sacred area would lie there in utter stillness for days at a time like animals in a lair. And the priests would take care of them, initiate them into the mysteries; for anyone else the area was deadly.

So the very same passage that throws so much light on the tradition about a line of healers from Velia also happens to be strangely relevant to Velia's most famous citizen: Parmenides.

And yet really there's nothing strange about this at all. For a long time—and long before the discoveries at Velia were ever made—historians noticed the way that Parmenides' account of his mythical journey connects him with incubation and with people who were experts at incubation: with people who justified their teachings on the basis of journeys they made into another world, who saw it as their job to bring back what they found and describe what they learned.

Making the connection between them and Parmenides is nothing new. The trouble is knowing what to do with it. When it has been acknowledged it's only acknowledged reluctantly. It couldn't possibly be relevant to the man known as the founder of western logic; the implications are far too great for how we understand ourselves and the origins of the culture we live in.

For a long time the significance of incubatory traditions in the ancient world has been lost. We assume the ideas that shaped western culture are just ideas, that it doesn't matter where they came from. We have no room for other states of consciousness—above all no time for anything to do with death. And yet no amount of explaining away Parmenides' journey, of taking the pieces we want and ignoring the rest, can cover up his connection with those people.

You can call them magicians if you want because that's exactly what they were, except that then there was no difference between mysticism and magic. The Greeks weren't always sure what to call them—these people with a mysterious wisdom who were never quite what they seemed, who appeared to have died while still alive.

But there was one particular name that fitted them perfectly. The name was Iatromantis.

Ecstasy

THEY DISCOVERED IT IN 1960. IT WAS LYING near the building with the hidden gallery where the Oulis inscriptions had been found.

Those three inscriptions for the Oulis healers were all engraved in the same style, parts of the same series. This was different: a block of marble with the vaguest remains of what once had been a public offering of thanks.

Carefully it was labelled for the official records—'Inventory number 20067, November 2nd 1960'—and put away. It wasn't even made public knowledge for another ten years. The delay was appropriate.

On the middle of the piece of marble you could just about make out the remains of three words. Nowadays three words are nothing. On an inscription like this they meant as much as a whole book.

The trouble is it wasn't the book that had been expected. Ever since the Oulis inscriptions were discovered people had passionately been hoping to find the proof of an ancient medical tradition in Italy, a tradition that would rival the famous school of Hippocrates. And really they'd found far more than that. But this fragment of marble was to prove nothing but an embarrassment—something to leave aside, mention as little as possible and be done with. For what it points to has no place on the map of our understanding.

THE THREE WORDS WERE

Ouliadês
Iatromantis
Apollo.

Ouliadês is more or less exactly the same word as Oulis, just a longer form of the name. Literally it means 'son of Oulios'. The connection with Apollo—the healing Apollo, Apollo Oulios—is implicit in the word itself; it would be crystal clear even if Apollo wasn't also mentioned, as he is, on the inscription.

Now, with one example of Ouliadês and three of Oulis, there could be no doubt. These people at Velia were maintainers of a cult of Apollo: priests of the god, his 'sons' and descendants, carriers of his name.

But the word Ouliadês isn't just a longer form of the name Oulis. It also has a longer history; can be traced back further in time. And this makes it easier to see what parts of the Greek world it had the closest links with.

The place where it was most popular of all was one particular area of Anatolia. That was the mountainous region to the south of Phocaea called Caria—the same Caria where Apollo Oulios was worshipped, where Apollo's title Phôleutêrios came from, where it was natural to compare lying down at an incubation shrine with lying down in a *phôleos* or lair.

So once again the Velian inscriptions were pointing back to the East, back to Anatolia, preserving engraved on stone the old traditions Phocaeans once shared in common with the Carians.

AND THEN there's the next word.

A Iatros is a healer; a Iatromantis is a healer of a very particular kind. He's a healer who's a prophet, a healer who heals through prophecy. But this isn't to say much at all unless we understand what prophecy used to mean.

Nowadays we think it has to do with telling the future. And yet that's just the result of centuries spent trivializing what for the Greeks was something very different. It used to mean giving a voice to what doesn't have a voice, meant acting as a mouthpiece for the divine. It all had to do with being able to contact and then talk from another level of consciousness.

The greatest prophets in ancient Greece were as famous for looking into the past and into the present as they were for looking into the future. They were able to see things in the present that are so obvious we miss them, and see the things in the past that hold us down and hold us back.

Healers known as Iatromantis worked in the same way. For them the prophecy was what came first—the ability to look behind the scenes, see what others don't. The healing followed as a matter of course.

That's not to say they didn't use techniques. They did. They were famous for their use of incantations: for chanting or repeating words in a way that can seem awkward or senseless but that has a certain effect, is able to induce a change in someone who says or hears them. And they used techniques of breath control to help break the hold of the senses, create access to an awareness beyond space and time.

For they operated on a level where nothing is at all the way it seems. As far as they were concerned the things we need to be healed of are often things we're not even aware of; and the knowledge we think we have of what's right for us or wrong with us is part of the ignorance we need to be healed of.

Their knowledge was entirely different from what knowledge is to us. And they got it from incubation. The basic function of a Phôlarchos or Lord of the Lair—that was their function as well. They were experts at working with dreams and through dreams: at listening to them, learning from them, healing with them. Iatromantis and Phôlarchos, like Oulis and Ouliadês, were two names pointing to the same thing.

And there's one other factor that all these different titles share in common. Just like the name Ouliadês, Iatromantis was a word that had the closest of links with Apollo. Greeks applied it either to Apollo himself or to someone they considered his son.

THERE'S ONE ASPECT of incubation that's easy to overlook. It's so basic but so subtle that it's almost always missed.

To most people nowadays a dream is nothing. It's just a dream and that's that. And yet for people in the ancient world there were dreams and there were dreams. Some were meaningful, others weren't; and some could take you into another kind of reality altogether.

If you look at the old accounts of incubation you can still read the amazement as people discovered that the state they'd entered continued regardless of whether they were asleep or awake, whether they opened their eyes or shut them. Often you find the mention of a state that's like being awake but different from being awake, that's like sleep but not sleep: that's neither sleep nor waking. It's not the waking state, it's not an ordinary dream and it's not dreamless sleep. It's something else, something in between.

People weren't bothered about giving it a name. They were more concerned with the experience than with trying to define it; and besides, for them the experience was an initiation into another world, a mystery. It was best just to say what it's not. If we want to we can talk about ecstasy or trance or a cataleptic state or suspended animation, but these are only ways of shooting in the dark. They say more about the physical body than about the state itself.

A Iatromantis was someone who was a master of this state of awareness. Waking is a form of consciousness, dreaming is another. And yet this is what we can live for a thousand years but never discover, what we can theorize or speculate about and never even come close to—consciousness itself.

It's what holds everything together and doesn't change. Once you experience this consciousness you know what it is to be neither asleep nor awake, neither alive nor dead, and to be at home not only in this world of the senses but in another reality as well.

A IATROMANTIS was concerned with indivisible oneness. His concern was very practical. What for us are impossible barriers were, for him, just places to put his feet. When you become familiar with a world beyond the senses, space and time don't hold much reality any more.

For the Greeks the god of this other state of awareness was Apollo. In his consciousness space and time mean nothing. He can see or be anywhere; past and future are as present as the present is for us. And so he was a god of ecstasy, trance, cataleptic states—of states that take you somewhere. There was a single word in Greek to express this; it meant 'taken by Apollo'.

Apollo's ecstasy was different from the ecstasy of Dionysus. There was nothing wild or disturbing about it. It was intensely private, for the individual and the individual alone. And it happened in such stillness that anyone else might hardly notice it or could easily mistake it for something else. But in this total stillness there was total freedom at another level.

On that other level the freedom from space and time is simply a fact. Doubting it doesn't affect it in the slightest, and neither does believing it: beliefs or doubts don't touch there. To convey a sense of this freedom, one name given to those priests of Apollo was 'skywalker'— a term used as far east as Tibet and Mongolia in just the same way.

Because the state of consciousness they knew is beyond time and space isn't to say that it's separate from time and space: by its very nature it's separate from separation. This has become so difficult to appreciate. Either we deny the existence of other states of awareness, or else we put them in a hierarchy somewhere out of reach. And yet the separation is only in our own minds.

These people didn't exist independent of the physical world, and their freedom showed through at every level of their existence. It's no accident that they came from the towns and areas of Greece most famous for daring and adventure, for contacts with foreigners, for long-distance travel. What's also significant is the way all of them either lived on the eastern edges of the Greek world—the Black Sea, Anatolia, Crete—or were born into families that had emigrated from there.

And so many things about them are so close to the shamanic traditions of Central Asia or Siberia that the similarities have been noticed time and time again. Nowadays this tends to create a problem. Most historians have their particular field of interest, are afraid of what lies outside. They like to say the Iatromantis is a purely Greek phenomenon and dismiss the similarities as a coincidence. But they're not a coincidence at all.

The particular kind of techniques used by magical healers in Crete simply confirms what was already discovered long ago: the closeness of Crete's contacts with Babylonians and Mesopotamia. And even more significant are the earliest Greek reports about Iatromantis figures—reports about how they'd travel up to and down from regions far to the north and east of Greece, how they'd pass through areas inhabited by Iranian tribes that were shamanic cultures in their own right and then on into Siberia and Central Asia.

Just a few traces survive of the poetry those people wrote describing their own journeys. But those traces are informative enough. They contain clear evidence of familiarity with Iranian languages as well as with the myths of Central Asia, Mongolia, Tibet. And that's only a part of the picture. Objects and inscriptions have also been found that show a continuity of shamanic traditions stretching all the way from the boundaries of Greece across Asia to the Himalayas and Tibet, Nepal and India.

WE THINK NOW of East and West. But then there were no real lines to be drawn. The oneness experienced by the Iatromantis on another level of awareness left its mark in the physical world. Even to talk about influence is to limit the reality of what was one vast network of nomads, of travellers, of individuals who lived in time and space but also were in touch with something else.

The way so many of the stories and practices associated with the Iatromantis in Greece have their exact parallels among shamans, and the way they keep occurring in the traditions of Indian yoga as well: this is more than a coincidence. What would soon be covered over and rationalized in Greece was preserved and developed in India. What in the West had been an aspect of mystery, of initiation, became classified and formalized in the East. And there the state glimpsed or experienced by Greeks—the state that could be called a dream but isn't an ordinary dream, that's like being awake but isn't being awake, that's like being asleep but isn't—had its own names. Sometimes it was simply referred to as the 'fourth', *turîya*. It became better known by the title of *samâdhi*.

Nothing would be easier than to think these traditions never took root in the West, or to believe that even if they did they were never of any importance for the history of western culture. But that's not the case. Just one of the people whose poetry has repeatedly been mentioned over the past century—without anyone quite understanding the why or the how—as an example of shamanic poetry in the West is Parmenides.

And in spite of the links they had with Persephone, the god of those Greek shamans was Apollo.

The Sound of Piping

FOR CENTURIES PEOPLE HAVE BEEN UPSET WITH Parmenides because he wrote a poem.

It was Aristotle who already made things very clear a long time ago: a philosopher's job is to speak as plainly as possible, call a spade a spade. As far as he was concerned, philosophy and poetry don't mix. A poem by a philosopher is simply doomed from the start.

Later on, philosophers found Parmenides' poem extremely obscure. Many of them were Platonists: for them Plato was a far greater authority than Parmenides ever could be and it was Plato's dialogues that presented the true Parmenides. Parmenides' own poetry was just a clumsy second best—a bad attempt at saying in verse what he would have been much better advised to discuss in prose.

And that's the way things stayed. You still find people complaining today about how bad he was at saying what he should have said: about how it's so 'hard to excuse Parmenides' choice of verse as a medium for his philosophy'.

But there's one problem with all of this. If you look closely at the poem itself, you start to see it was written with consummate craft. The skill is so clear when you care to look. Scholars in the last few years have been amazed to discover that Parmenides created some of the most powerful and haunting lines of poetry ever written.

His ear for sound was remarkable. He used it carefully to produce specific effects. He felt free to break the rules of poetic metre, to commit what easily could be considered mistakes. This wasn't because he was careless, or clumsy, but because it allowed him to express dramatically through sound and unexpected rhythm the point that he wanted to make.

The flow of his poetry is unusual. Normally Greek poets liked to lead up to a climax at the end of each line. With Parmenides it's the other way round. That could seem like a weakness until you realize it has to do with the fundamental nature of his poem. Instead of exploding outwards into countless details it implodes: draws us inwards, back into the depths of ourselves.

There's also a special delicacy in his choice of images and combinations of words—a special sense of humour. But his subtlety, his fondness for ambiguity, the ways he plays with sound and meaning, are much more than poetic skill. For the language he uses isn't an ordinary one. It's the language of oracles and riddles, of hints and double meanings, addressed to those who know or really want to know: the language of initiation.

PARMENIDES does something very peculiar at the start of his poem. He keeps repeating himself, using the same words over and over again.

Hardly anyone notices, but that's not surprising. There's a kind of unwritten rule in studying the first of the western philosophers: never start at the point where they start. That would mean having to take their concerns and interests seriously, having to understand them on their own terms. So people start in the middle instead—anywhere rather than right at the beginning. The trouble is that unless you start at the beginning everything immediately becomes confused.

It's as if you wanted to go and visit someone to hear him talk; but as soon as you're there you sit down, cross one leg over the other and start imagining what you think the person will say later on instead of listening to what he has to say now. It would have been better never to have gone.

There are just a couple of scholars who have noticed how Parmenides keeps on repeating words. They talk about how 'naive' and 'amateurish' a poet he was, how much 'carelessness' he shows; dismiss his 'awkward and pointless repetition of the same word' as a classic example of 'expressive failure'.

But the fact is that in the first four lines of the original Greek he uses the word for 'carry' four times. And that's only the beginning. A poor poet could perhaps repeat the same word once and it would be an accident. This is no accident.

And it isn't awkward or naive. To write a poem in those days wasn't anything at all like writing in prose. Greek poets followed strict rules: either they took the greatest care to avoid repeating words or they used repetition for a very specific reason. Even with a poet far less skilful than Parmenides, using the same word four times in as many lines would be quite deliberate.

This type of insistent repetition wasn't common in the ancient world. But it existed. It was a technique for creating an incantatory effect, and the purpose of the incantation was magical. Either it could be used for healing or it could be used to draw people into another state of consciousness. So right at the start of his poem Parmenides is drawing his listener into the world of incantations and magic, of healing and other states of awareness—the world of the Iatromantis.

ONE OF THE MOST OBVIOUS TECHNIQUES he uses in describing his journey is to keep switching the time of the events. At one moment he presents it as a journey that happened in the past; then he describes it as happening right now, in the present. This shifting between past and present was a popular method with Greek writers for evoking a scene, for making it immediate and living and real.

But Parmenides' use of repetition is something more than that. It doesn't just evoke the journey. It's a way of actually creating the journey: of inducing the state that makes it possible.

The fact that he starts off by repeating the word for 'carry' isn't a coincidence. The repetition of the word for 'carry' is what carries. Through his words he draws the listener, and the words he uses are words of power.

Philosophy has come to mean discussion, trying to use the mind to reach meaning with the help of words—and yet never really succeeding. But in Parmenides' time things were very different. Then the words of a philosopher were words of power. They weren't words in search of meaning but words that contained their own meaning inside them.

There were philosophers who made the situation quite clear: they explained how the words in their poems were seeds that were meant to be absorbed so they could grow and transform the nature of the hearer, give rise to a different awareness. And just a couple of those words whispered in your ear can stop you in your tracks, change your life forever.

People have been fascinated by these poems for ages: can't help being drawn to the fragments of them that still survive. They try to rationalize them, and when necessary decide to change their meaning here or there to give them a more acceptable sense.

And yet they don't appreciate the source of the fascination. Those poems are incantatory texts. Their writers were magicians and sorcerers.

THERE COULD SEEM TO BE one very real problem in making sense of the way Parmenides talks about his journey. This is the fact that, right at the start of his poem, he describes himself as a 'man who knows' even before he reaches the goddess or receives the knowledge she has to give him. If he already knows before he makes the journey there's no real reason to make it at all.

The answer to the problem is so simple once you see what he's saying, and what he's doing. As a 'man who knows' he's an initiate—someone who's able to enter another world, to die before dying. And the knowledge of how to do that is what leads him to the wisdom given by Persephone.

It's exactly the same as in the case of another descent to the world of the dead: the famous descent by Orpheus. One fine scholar once explained Orpheus' situation perfectly. 'He doesn't need to ask the divinities of the underworld for a knowledge he already has because it was the effectiveness of this knowledge of his that allowed him to make the journey into their world in the first place.' And Orpheus' knowledge was the initiate's knowledge of incantations, of the magic power of words—of poetry 'that has an effect capable even of reaching into the world of the dead'.

Parmenides' words aren't theory or discussion. They're a language that achieves what it says. And his use of repetition isn't bad poetry; isn't amateurish or careless. It demonstrates in a direct and tangible form what Orpheus was believed to have done in myth. For this is his song.

FOR US a song and a road are very different things. But in the language of ancient Greek epic poetry the word for 'road' and the word for 'song', *oimos* and *oimê*, are almost identical. They're linked, have the same origin.

Originally the poet's song was quite simply a journey into another world: a world where the past and future are as accessible and real as the present. And his journey was his song. Those were the times when the poet was a magician, a shaman.

Parmenides' incantatory technique certainly has its links with the mythology of Orpheus—and with the shamanic origins of Orphic tradition in the far northern and eastern corners of Greece. But it also points back to what for a long time historians have realized are the roots of Greek epic poetry itself: its roots in the language of shamans.

The words shamans use as they enter the state of ecstasy evoke the things they speak about. The poems they sing don't only describe their journeys; they're what makes the journeys happen.

And shamans have always used repetition as a matter of course to invoke a consciousness quite different from our ordinary awareness: a consciousness where something else starts to take over. The repetition is what draws them into another world, away from all the things we know.

IN A SENSE, those who notice Parmenides' practice of repeating words and then dismiss it as awkward or naive have missed the point entirely. But in another sense they're perfectly right in what they say.

In the modern world repetition and naivety go hand in hand. Sophistication is the highest virtue—the search for endless variety, for ways to keep scattering our longing in entertainments and distractions, in different things to do and say. Even the attempts we make to improve ourselves, become wiser or more interesting or successful, are just methods of running from the hollowness we all feel inside.

So we get everything upside down and back to front, mistaking sophistication for maturity and hardly noticing that there's nothing more repetitious than the desire for variety.

It needs a tremendous focus, an immense intensity, to break through the wall of appearances that surround us and that we think of as reality. Most people paint their wall in different colours and then imagine they're free.

But what's extraordinary is that the crucial thing we need for breaking free is already inside us: our longing. And the voice of our longing is repetition, insistently calling out to what's beyond anything we're familiar with or even understand.

To begin with, it can seem such a challenge not to be distracted and pulled to the right or the left—just to keep to a line of utter simplicity that's able to draw us into another world. Every appearance seems marshalled against us, and all we have to hold on to is the insistent repetition of our own longing. But then something very subtle happens.

As you start being drawn behind appearances you begin to touch the bare bones of existence, to discover another reality behind the scenes. And you can never take anything at face value any more.

You start to see the underlying principles behind events, the basic patterns that keep repeating themselves time after time; and repetition begins to show itself in everything. Instead of appearances being an obstacle, they help you on your journey. And everything starts speaking with the voice of your own longing.

That's why the repetition in Parmenides' account of his journey soon spreads to all the details he describes. At first it's just a matter of the way he's carried and continuously carried 'as far as longing can reach'. But then he starts explaining how object after object that he encounters on his journey is 'held fast'; and in whatever moves he keeps seeing the same pattern of spinning in a circle. The chariot wheels spin on the axle, the doors spin on their axles as they open into the underworld.

Everything becomes simpler and simpler—less unique, an echo of something else—until gradually you see where all this repetition of detail is leading. Each single thing that exists is being reduced to a small part of the pattern created by the interplay of night and day, of light and darkness. For those are the fundamental opposites that, as Parmenides will explain later on, repeat themselves endlessly in different combinations to produce the universe we think we live in.

The way he reduces appearances to the basic opposites of light and dark, night and day, has often been noticed. But this reduction isn't some philosophical theory. It's the result of travelling behind appearances to what for ancient Greek poets are the roots of existence: into the darkness where all light comes from, where everything merges with its opposite.

And it's all very practical—very real. This is what happens when instead of trying to run away from repetition you find the courage to face it, go through it. Then you arrive at something that's beyond any sort of repetition because it's completely still and timeless.

THERE ARE SOME THINGS that matter more than we realize, but we can find a thousand reasons for dismissing them.

Usually we're so full of ideas and opinions, of fears and expectations, that we can hardly hear anything beyond the noise of our own thoughts; and so we miss the most important things. Or even worse, we just dismiss them as insignificant. It's not for nothing that people weren't allowed even to listen to Pythagoras' teachings until they had practised being silent for years.

There's one simple detail in Parmenides' account of his journey to the underworld that's so easy to miss. During the whole of his journey there's no mention at all of any noise—apart from one single sound. That's the sound the chariot makes as the daughters of the Sun draw him along: 'the sound of a pipe'.

And this is where we're brought face to face with one of the most obvious examples of repetition. For after Parmenides mentions the sound of the pipe he uses the same word again to explain how the huge doors spin open, rotating in hollow tubes or 'pipes'.

This use of the word is extraordinary. It's the only time in the whole Greek language that it's ever applied to doors or parts of doors, and scholars have pointed out that Parmenides must have chosen it for a particular reason: not simply to describe what the doors look like but also to give a sense of the sound they make. On his journey everything that moves has to do with the sound or the appearance of pipes. The doors with their axles imitate the axle on the chariot, the spinning of the doors copies the spinning of the chariot's wheels, and there's just the suggestion—nothing more—that the sound of the chariot is echoed by the sound of the opening doors.

That's the way repetition works. It blurs differences, blends one thing into another. It can only be explained up to a certain point because in fact it has to do with another kind of awareness. And so you're faced with an apparent choice. Either you stand back, and walk away, or you allow yourself to be taken.

THE WORD for 'pipe' that Parmenides keeps using is *syrinx*. It had a very particular spread of meanings. *Syrinx* was the name either for a musical instrument or for the part of an instrument that makes a piping, whistling sound—the sound called *syrigmos*. But there's one aspect of these words that you have to bear in mind: for Greeks this sound of piping and whistling was also the sound of the hissing made by snakes.

It would be so simple to dismiss as totally insignificant the fact that this piping, whistling, hissing noise is the only sound Parmenides associates with his journey to another world—except for one small matter.

Ancient Greek accounts of incubation repeatedly mention certain signs that mark the point of entry into another world: into another state of awareness that's neither waking nor sleep. One of the signs is that you become aware of a rapid spinning movement. Another is that you hear the powerful vibration produced by a piping, whistling, hissing sound.

In India exactly the same signs are described as the prelude to entering *samâdhi*, the state beyond sleep and waking. And they're directly related to the process known as the awakening of *kundalinî*—of the 'serpent power' that's the basic energy in all creation but that's almost completely asleep in human beings. When it starts waking up it makes a hissing sound.

The parallels between standard Indian accounts of the process and Parmenides' account of his journey are obvious enough; specialists in Indian traditions have written about them and discussed them. But what hasn't been noticed is that the particular sound mentioned by Parmenides also happens to be the sound made by a hissing snake.

PROBABLY THE MOST FAMOUS magical text of all from the ancient Greek world is written on a large papyrus, stored away now in a vast old Paris library. It's part of a strange story that really hasn't been told and possibly never will be.

As well as giving examples for how to use the magical repetition of words to go into a state of trance, it has a section sometimes referred to as the recipe for immortality. The recipe is strictly esoteric, only for transmission from a spiritual 'father' to his adopted 'son'. It's a recipe for going through an inner process of death—for being brought almost to the point of physical extinction, far from 'any human being or living thing'—so that the initiate can be born into a world beyond space and time. And it involves making a cosmic journey while in another state of consciousness to the real origin of all human life: the sun.

Repeatedly the initiate is told by the 'father' magician that on the different stages of his journey he has to keep producing a piping, whistling, hissing sound—the sound of a *syrinx*. There's a whole number of reasons why this was so important. First, magicians used to make that particular hissing sound as part of an exercise in breath control to help them enter an altered state of awareness. And second, the sound of a *syrinx* was a call for silence. This is something that makes sense even on a very obvious level when you consider how hissing or whistling at people is still a way of silencing them. To ancient mystics and magicians the journey into a greater reality was a journey made through silence, in silence and into silence. The noise of a *syrinx* is the ultimate password. It's the sound of silence.

But the recipe for immortality is also categorical about one detail. Before an initiate can be accepted in the realm of the gods he first has to convince them he belongs there. The way he's told to do this is to say the words 'I too am a star, wandering around together with you, shining out of the depths.' And this is when he has to keep making the sound of a *syrinx*.

It's not hard to see why. Greek mystical texts explain that this hissing or piping sound, this sound of silence, is the sound of creation. It's the noise made by the stars, by the planets as they coil and spin in their orbits. Sometimes, depending on how loud or quiet it is, you can hear it in the whistling or roaring of the wind. There are also traditions that say this is what's meant by the famous harmony of the spheres: the sound Pythagoras once heard in a state of ecstasy, in total stillness.

And it's no ordinary sound. An Anatolian oracle of Apollo, delivered in the form of a poem from one of his temples that was built just above a cave leading down to the underworld, states the matter very clearly.

It explains how after a person comes into contact with the source of this sound then 'there's no tearing one's heart away, because it allows no separation'.

THERE'S ONE CENTRAL KEY to understanding the recipe for immortality.

This is the initiate's approach to the sun. The sun is his god, his 'god of gods'. It's through the sun that he's born again—and for that to happen he has to travel in the path of the sun itself. One of his names in the mysteries was 'sun-runner'. This was almost the last stage of initiation, and was the name given to someone who's able to ride in the chariot of the sun.

So it's no surprise to find that making the sound of a *syrinx* also has a very special link with the sun. And yet the vividness of the details in the recipe that help to explain the link is quite amazing. For an extraordinary picture is presented to the initiate of how in reality the sun has a tube hanging down from it: a tube that's not just an ordinary tube, but a musical pipe.

This link between the sun and musical pipes isn't at all unique. You find it mentioned in other Greek and

Latin texts as well; one Orphic hymn even gives the sun the title of *syriktês*, 'the piper'. And it doesn't take much to see how closely this is all connected to Parmenides' account of his journey—to the persistent sound of piping as he's guided along the route of the sun, in the chariot of the sun, by the daughters of the sun.

The texts that mention these things were written in the centuries after Christ, certainly a long time after Parmenides. But this type of tradition doesn't come or go in the space of a day. Writings on papyrus like the example now at Paris were found in the same country where they were produced: in Egypt. And yet they're not really original documents, just copies made from copies. In them different ideas and practices are mixed, blended together; and there's a whole history to the traditions they contain.

Some of the ideas are Egyptian. But there are also tell-tale details that point back over hundreds of years to one particular area and period of the ancient world— back to Italy and Sicily in the fifth century BC. You can still trace the outlines of the journeys once made by those magical and mystical traditions, at a time when Greeks were starting to leave the homes they had created in the west so they could emigrate to the new centres of culture in Egypt.

And as for those links between the sun and the sound of piping, the basic facts are very simple.

Scattered through passages in the magical papyri concerned with initiation into the mysteries of the sun you find references to Apollo and a huge snake—and to the magical power of the snake's hissing. One of the first people in modern times ever to study the papyri already perceived the essentials over a hundred years ago. He saw that these references point back to ancient traditions from Delphi: traditions about Apollo's fight with a snake of prophecy that used to guard the oracle there for the powers of earth and night, right next to a chasm opening into the underworld.

But he also noticed that they agree most closely with forms of those Delphic traditions best known from southern Italy.

I*T'S EASY TO ASSUME* that the Delphic myth of Apollo fighting the snake is a straightforward case of a battle between the opposites—of Apollo as a celestial god overcoming the powers of earth and darkness. But something needs to be understood.

Alongside the intimacy of Apollo's links with the underworld, there's another aspect of him that also has been pushed into the dark. That's his connection with snakes. In ritual and in art snakes were sacred to him. Even in the case of the myth about the snake he fought and killed at Delphi, he didn't destroy it just to get it out of the way. On the contrary, its body was buried at the centre of his shrine. He killed it so he could absorb, appropriate, the prophetic powers that the snake represents.

It was the same in other places. At Rome he was known for approaching people who came to visit his great incubation shrine by appearing to them in the middle of the night as a snake. This could seem unusual until you notice how normal it was for Greeks to describe him as assuming the form of a snake.

And it was only natural for the same pattern to keep repeating itself with Apollo's son Asclepius when—in the centuries after Parmenides—he gradually took over the healing powers that used to belong to his father. Asclepius would come, followed by hissing snakes, to people who approached him; or he'd come in the form of a snake. The hissing, *syrigmos*, was the sound of his presence.

There have been scholars so determined to present Asclepius as nothing but a mild and gentle god that when they come to translate the words describing this side of him they simply miss them out. But the old texts are quite clear. If people weren't already used to the sound of his presence then it would terrify them—like the sound of wild nature at its wildest when you're all on your own— as they lay sleeping or in the state that's neither waking nor sleep.

THE ORACLE AT DELPHI used to be the centre of centres for the Greeks' worship of Apollo.

It was considered the navel of the earth. In the days when Greeks had sailed west to create new colonies for themselves in Italy they used to depend on it—and on its traditions—for their lives and for their futures.

At every great Delphic festival Apollo's fight with the snake was dramatized, put to music. The drama became a crucial part of initiation into mysteries of Apollo not just at Delphi but across the rest of the Greek world. And it was no secret that when Apollo killed the snake he was only a child, a *kouros*; or that the initiate who acted out his role had to be a *kouros*, too.

The climax to the whole drama was the last act. This was the one that described how Apollo came to power, and it was called after the musical instrument used for imitating the hissing of the snake: the *syrinx*.

That wasn't its only name. This final act was also known as *syrigmos*—a sound the Greeks usually weren't too fond of. But it was the sound made by Asclepius, as well as by the sun. And behind all that, as the sound of his victory over the power of darkness, it was sacred to Apollo.

Three

ΠΑ[.].ΕΝΕΙΔΗΣΠΥΡΗΤΟΣ
ΟΥΛΙΑΔΗΣΦΥΣΙΚΟΣ

Founding Hero

S EPTEMBER, 1962. VELIA.
Mario Napoli stumbled across it as he was searching through the same building with the hidden gallery where the Oulis inscriptions had been found. It was the answer to everyone's prayers.

Lying buried upside down in the ground, exactly where it had been left nineteen hundred years ago to prevent people falling into a small drainage ditch, was a block of marble with another inscription. But this time the inscription wasn't for some unknown person. It was for Parmenides.

Close by, Napoli found a statue of Asclepius—a carved snake climbing up the left side of the god's carved robe.

THE MARBLE BLOCK had been cracked and battered and misused. No trace seemed to survive of any head or statue of Parmenides that originally would have been attached to it. But the writing on the inscription could still be read very easily.

Parmeneides son of Pyres Ouliadês Physikos.

Even the form of the name, Parmeneides, was significant. In all the written sources handed down from antiquity his name was always given as Parmenides—except in just one ancient manuscript. Long ago specialists had guessed from this single manuscript that the real form of his name had been Parmeneides; now the inscription showed they were right.

And it was no news, either, that his father's name was Pyres. Many of the Greek and Roman writers who left reports about Parmenides' teaching had already mentioned the fact. But here, among all the other inscriptions from Velia with their consistent Anatolian background, the detail had a particular relevance of its own. Pyres was a very rare name in the ancient world—and yet it was a familiar one at Miletus, the famous Greek city in that area of Anatolia once known as Caria.

Just the same as with the spelling of Parmenides' own name, the inscription wasn't really offering anything new by mentioning his father. But suddenly the old, familiar facts were starting to take on a far wider meaning. Parmenides was becoming a man with a past in space as well as time: a past that linked him in every possible way to Anatolia.

Then there was the title Ouliadês.

This was new; it hadn't been found applied to Parmenides before. And as everybody quickly saw, it tied him in with the line of Oulis healers mentioned on the other inscriptions from Velia.

But those people weren't just ordinary healers. They were 'sons' and priests of Apollo, healers belonging to a world of Iatromantis figures concerned with incubation and dreams and ecstasy: a world of magicians who spoke in poetry and oracles and riddles, who used incantations to enter other states of consciousness.

Now this inscription was saying that Parmeneides was one of them.

THE LAST of the words started a furious debate as soon as the inscription was published.

Physikos is the origin of our word 'physicist'. It used to mean someone who's interested in the beginnings and the nature of the universe. But it's also the origin of the English 'physician': it could be a way of referring to doctors or healers, as well.

Some experts argued that here it just means Parmeneides was concerned with primordial realities and the way things came to be what they are. Others insisted that it means he's being presented as a doctor or physician, similar to the three Oulis healers.

And the argument was pointless. Both sides were wrong, both were right. 'Physician' and 'physicist', 'physics' and 'physical' are all modern versions of a word that used to mean much more than any of them. Instead of trying to choose which of these senses fits the inscription best we have to get back behind them, back to where they all come from.

A *physikos* was someone who's concerned with the basic principles of existence, who's able to touch the bare bones of what things are—and also use the knowledge that he finds. That's why it became a normal term for describing magicians and alchemists.

But here on the inscription from Velia it's applied to Parmeneides. And this isn't the only place where he's described the same way. In fact it was just about as common for writers to call him a *physikos* as it was to introduce him by mentioning the routine detail that his father's name was Pyres.

The reason is quite simple. In the ancient world *physikos* was a standard way of referring to the earliest of the philosophers. And there's the catch.

For a long while now the beginnings of western philosophy have been presented as purely a matter of intellectual speculation, of abstract ideas. But that's only a myth. Especially in Italy and Sicily the reality was very different. There philosophy had developed as something all-embracing, intensely practical. And this included the whole area of healing, except that healing then wasn't the same as it's now understood.

In fact you wouldn't be wrong if you were to say that the western rational medicine we're so familiar with came into being as a direct reaction against the earliest of those philosophers—against people like Parmeneides who assumed the role of *physikos*. Our modern image of doctors and healing was first shaped by Hippocrates; and the famous school he founded soon felt the need to define its aims by excluding from medicine anything that didn't specifically have to do with medicine. So it lashed out at those philosophers, attacking them because of the way they insisted that before you can really heal anyone you first have to know what men and women are in their deepest nature—what human beings are from the beginning, not just how they react to this or that condition.

And yet when Hippocratic writers adopted this position they weren't simply attacking theoretical philosophers. They saw themselves as attacking people who were their competitors, who were also healers in their own right.

They had every good reason for seeing things that way.

There used to be a famous tradition about Pythagoras, that he went around from city to city and town to town 'not to teach but to heal'. And the first great philosophical systems created in Italy and Sicily weren't theoretical products at all. Then knowledge of how the universe came into being, or of the elements that make up reality, was meant to have a practical application.

But above all it was bound up with healing—with getting one's own life in order on every possible level and helping other people get their lives in order as well.

The problem in understanding this link between philosophy and healing doesn't have anything to do with a lack of evidence. The evidence is there; the only problem is the blanket of silence that's been thrown over it. For there's one thing that makes the knowledge those early philosophers had so difficult to grasp and make sense of. This is the fact that it didn't have its origin in thinking or reasoning.

It came from the experience of other states of consciousness. Those philosophers, those people attacked in the Hippocratic writings, happen to have been Iatromantis figures: they were mystics and magicians. And as far as they were concerned there's no real healing until you come to discover what you are behind the world of the senses.

A TIME CAME—it was well before the inscription was carved for Parmeneides—when the word *physikos* started being used in a specifically medical context. It began being applied to people who were healers and doctors.

At least that's the way things seemed. But in fact the word was much more than an equivalent for 'physician' or 'healer'. It had a far wider scope.

You can still read the clearest of statements from ancient writers explaining that healing and medicine are just a tiny part of 'physic', of the fundamental understanding about reality and about what makes things the way they are. The term *physikos*—or *physicus* in Latin—was only applied to doctors when they started taking an interest in that greater world behind the world of medicine. And this is how things stayed right through to the Middle Ages and beyond.

So it's no surprise to find that, apart from everything else, Parmeneides' own poem contained detailed information on subjects like the growth of the foetus and sexual peculiarities and the nature of old age. And there's nothing to be surprised at in the way that he came to be quoted as an authority by the greatest medical experts in the ancient world, or that according to traditions about him transmitted from Alexandria at the tip of Egypt through to the Arab world—as well as in southern Italy itself down to the thirteenth century—he was known as the legendary head of a medical tradition who had healers for his successors. This was all a natural part of being a famous *physikos*.

And yet there's a twist to the story, the way that with someone like Parmeneides there always is.

For centuries this aspect of his teaching has hardly been noticed at all. Everything he had to say about these matters belonged to the last part of his poem: the part where the goddess describes the world we live in and declares that it's all a deception. By putting things this way he was almost inviting people not to take any of it seriously. And that's just what happened. The last part of the poem has been so neglected that only a few lines from it have even survived; the rest is lost, forgotten.

And certainly for Parmeneides birth and age and death were only illusions. But that's not to say he didn't care for them, or take them seriously. For it's when we don't take care of illusions that they start becoming real.

CALLING PARMENEIDES A *PHYSIKOS* was a way of creating a subtle difference between him and the healers called Oulis. It didn't mean he wasn't like them, that he wasn't concerned or involved with healing; on the contrary. But it was a way of saying he was something else, something more.

And that's not the only difference.

The age of the Parmeneides inscription, its style, the shape and size of the writing, the condition of the marble it was carved on—every detail was more or less exactly the same as on the inscriptions for the Oulis healers. But in this case something was missing. There was no year, no date.

People immediately realized that the absence of a date was just as significant as anything the inscription does say. And the reason for the absence is quite simple. In this case a date wasn't needed because Parmeneides himself represents the year zero: all the numbers on the other inscriptions—year 280, year 379, year 446—were being counted from him.

Century after century this line of healers had continued to exist, looking back to Parmeneides as its source and dating its existence from him. To measure the age of a tradition or institution by dating it from its founder was nothing unusual in the ancient world. It was normal to acknowledge and then worship the person as a hero, beginning from the moment when he died.

And there was one formal way of referring to such a person. This was to call him *hêrôs ktistês*, the founding hero.

NOWADAYS it could seem very strange for the founder of western philosophy to have been a priest. And it could seem even stranger for someone who's a priest also to be treated as a hero.

But in fact this isn't so strange at all. There are inscriptions from the ancient world that help to fill out a picture of chief priests being worshipped as heroes in their own right after they died. They were priests who had been responsible for giving out oracles of the gods, who became famous in the region where they'd lived either for founding new traditions or for creating new forms of old ones. And this was especially true in the case of people who had been priests of Apollo.

The plainest evidence of all for these founding figures comes from the western coastal regions of Anatolia. Sometimes the priest is a figure lost in the mists of legend; sometimes he's a clearly historical person. But what's constant is a chain of succession created by 'sons' of Apollo, tracing its existence generation after generation back to the founding hero. For the links between heroes and the worship of Apollo were very close.

And that's not even to mention the practice of creating special shrines for Iatromantis figures when they died and then treating them as heroes—heroes in the sense of people who had something extraordinary about them, something divine, who through the lives they lived had gone beyond the limits of ordinary human possibility or experience.

BIT BY BIT AND PIECE BY PIECE the discoveries at Velia were pulling Parmeneides away from the usual image of him as a dry intellectual into a world of a totally different order. And that world was a reality: it's only to us that it seems unreal.

But even so, the Velian inscriptions were simply telling one part of the story. For really all of them together were just one single fragment of a far larger puzzle. And there were even stranger things to come, because this wasn't the end of Parmeneides' connections with heroes—and neither was it the beginning.

The Line

T HERE'S A PECULIAR PIECE OF INFORMATION about Parmeneides that's been known for a long, long time.

It's such a small detail: something you mightn't even notice. It's that he adopted his successor, Zeno, as his son.

And as always, we're faced with a choice. Either we can walk right past the evidence, or we can follow it wherever it leads.

THE WHOLE SUBJECT OF ADOPTION in the ancient world is a strange affair. Adopting someone two and a half thousand years ago wasn't the same as it is now. The issue of how old you were really didn't matter; the person you adopted could be grown up, too. Most of those taboos we have about adopted people contacting their natural parents—they simply didn't exist. And often the reasons behind adoption were religious. For it had a profound connection with the mysteries.

Just how usual or unusual the practice used to be among ancient Greeks isn't so easy to say. A lot depended on particular regions; on local laws and lawgivers. And apart from the factors of geography or space there's also the factor of time. Ways of referring to people and to their ancestors changed over the centuries, and this meant that clear statements acknowledging someone was someone else's adopted child only started becoming standard at quite a late period in history—even though the actual practice of adoption was far, far older.

And yet in terms of solid evidence, in terms of the sheer numbers of examples still known, there's one general area where adoption among the Greeks was more common than anywhere else.

That was the western coastal regions of Anatolia— especially Caria as well as the islands lying offshore from Caria. And the plainest evidence of all comes from the inscriptions left behind by the great priestly families who used to live there.

But Anatolia also happens to have been a place where priestly traditions went hand in hand with the practice of healing. That's how things stayed from the earliest times right through to the end of the classical world. Anatolian families of priests often tended to be families of healers as well; and this connection is particularly clear in cases where teachers decided to adopt or foster their successors.

As you'd expect, the process of being adopted into these families was tied up with initiation. In fact so much romance and mystique became associated with the process that writers of ancient novels loved to describe it. Here was a perfect way of giving local colour to the stories they set in the exotic coastal cities of western Anatolia—stories about loss and discovery, about unexpectedly being recognized and rescued and brought back to life when everything had seemed beyond hope.

THERE HAVEN'T BEEN TOO MANY HISTORIANS prepared to stop and pay attention to such a little detail as the one about Parmeneides adopting Zeno. But as for the few who have been, it was only natural that they'd try to understand it by drawing comparisons. And—even quite independently of any knowledge about a Velian line of healers tracing its existence back to Parmeneides—one particular comparison seemed highly suggestive.

This was with the line of ancient healers that made up the most famous medical school of all: the school of Hippocrates, situated on the island of Cos just off the mainland from Caria. There the basic principle of teacher adopting pupil was so important that it's even referred to explicitly in the Hippocratic Oath.

But that's not to say the idea here of teachers adopting their pupils and considering them a part of their family was unique to healers. On the contrary, scholars have already noticed that the real origins of the special significance Hippocratic tradition attached to this link between teacher and pupil don't have anything to do with medical practice. They lie in the mysteries.

In fact it's no coincidence that Hippocrates happens to have been an Asklepiadês or 'son of Asclepius', just as Parmeneides was an Ouliadês or son of Apollo Oulios: that behind Hippocrates himself hovers the shadow of a lineage tracing its ancestry all the way back to Asclepius.

And behind the Asclepius worshipped on Cos hovers the shadow of another god—the god who was his father, who used to share his healing shrines with him, who's mentioned even before Asclepius right at the start of the Hippocratic Oath. That was Apollo, sometimes known on the island as Apollo Oulios.

ANOTHER COMPARISON was also waiting to be made. But this one was even more obvious; and it brings everything much nearer back to home.

There's a certain group of people that ancient writers used to say Parmeneides and Zeno had the closest of connections with. Guessing which group that was shouldn't be too hard: it was the Pythagoreans in southern Italy. In fact both of them were quite often referred to as Pythagoreans themselves.

Nowadays it's normal not to want to take these connections seriously. Parmeneides and Zeno were such creative, original writers; and the notion of belonging to a group or system, especially a mystical group like the Pythagoreans, seems so incompatible with anything original or creative.

And yet that's to miss one crucial point. Originally Pythagoreans weren't so concerned with fixed ideas or doctrines as they were with something quite different: something that didn't just tolerate creativity and originality but encouraged them, nurtured them, guided people to their source. This is why the Pythagorean tradition managed to stay so elusive—why it was so open-ended, blending with other traditions, defying our modern ideas of orthodoxy or self-definition.

The evidence is still there to show how highly valued individuality and creative freedom once were in Pythagorean circles. That can sound such a paradox to us; we're so used to thinking of religious groups or sects as made up of brainwashed, mindless men and women. But as a matter of fact this is one of the least paradoxical things about Pythagoreanism. The problem is simply a problem of understanding. Originality and creativity have come to be imagined in such superficial terms, and the cult of the individual has developed into such an effective form of brainwashing, that it's not easy any longer even to conceive of anything else.

Becoming a Pythagorean wasn't a casual matter of learning something and leaving. The process touched aspects of the human being so remote from ordinary experience that it can only be described in abstract terms, even though there was nothing abstract about it.

You could say it was about what we fear most. It was about facing silence, about having no choice but to give up every kind of opinion and theory that we cling to, about not even finding anything to replace them for years on end.

Your whole life was turned upside down, from the inside out. And during this process the bond between teacher and disciple was essential. That's why it was seen as the relationship between a father and an adopted child. Your teacher became your parent—just the same as through initiation into the mysteries. Becoming a Pythagorean meant being adopted, being introduced into a great family.

The background to the type of adoption practised by Pythagoreans was very simple. Essentially it was a process of rebirth: of becoming a child again, a *kouros*. And in this setting there was more to being adopted than meets the eye.

The physical facts of heredity were never wiped out or cancelled. They continued to apply and have their obvious validity. But alongside that, something else was created.

The adoption wasn't just a part of a mystery. It was a mystery in itself. It meant being initiated into a family that exists on another level from anything we're used to. Outwardly all the links with the past still existed. And yet inwardly there was an awareness of belonging somewhere else more than it's ever possible to belong anywhere here —of being cared for more intimately than it's possible to be cared for by a human being.

As for the people who played the role of teacher and initiator, they could seem human enough. But the role they played was far more than the role of a human parent. They were the embodiments of another world. At their hands you died to everything you were, to everything you'd learned to cling to as though it was your whole existence. That's why they sometimes were referred to— in the cases where they were men—as 'true fathers'. And the emphasis was on the word 'true'. From the point of view of the mysteries the ordinary life we all know is only a first step, a preliminary to something else entirely.

Among early Pythagoreans the importance attached to this process of interaction between 'parent' and 'child', of transmission from one to the other, was fundamental. It led to ethical demands that were tremendous. And these demands weren't always formal requirements: often they had to be intuited instead. Even the Pythagorean legends still reflect the need that sometimes might be felt to be present physically at the teacher's deathbed when he died.

But behind the specifics there was one central fact. This was the fact that the teacher is a point of access to something beyond the teacher. And behind one teacher there's a whole line of teachers, one behind the other. The teaching was simply transmitted from generation to generation, one step at a time, often in secret and sometimes in circumstances of immense difficulty.

The result was utterly paradoxical. People's lives and even their deaths were surrendered to their teacher. And yet they surrendered to nothing. They became a part of a vast system; but through that system they found an extraordinary creativity. They became members of a family that was indescribably intimate—and totally impersonal.

Each teacher seemed to have a face but really was faceless: just one link in a chain of tradition reaching back to Pythagoras. And Pythagoras himself was nameless. Pythagoreans avoided mentioning him by name because his identity was a mystery—in the same way that they often avoided mentioning each other's names or the names of the gods. As far as they were concerned, Pythagoras wasn't only the man he had appeared to be.

They knew him as a son of Apollo or, quite simply, as Apollo himself.

AND THEN we come to Plato. For there's one other piece of information that also survives, buried away in his writings.

It's really rather extraordinary how he chose to talk about 'father Parmenides'—and about the possibility of patricide—at just the moment when he was trying to define the essence of his relationship to Parmeneides as one philosopher to another.

But this isn't only extraordinary. As a number of scholars have seen, it's significant too. Exactly the same form of address, 'father', that Plato uses for referring to Parmeneides was used by Pythagoreans when referring to the man who happened to be their teacher. It was also the standard title given to initiators into the ancient mysteries, as well as being the formal name for someone who reaches the very last stage of initiation.

And yet Plato doesn't say Parmeneides was his own father. He's more subtle and precise than that. Carefully he puts the reference to 'father Parmenides', along with the talk about patricide, into the mouth of one of the imaginary speakers in his dialogue. He doesn't even give the speaker a proper name but simply presents him as a citizen of Velia—or Elea, as Plato preferred to say. And he quaintly refers to him as the 'Eleatic stranger'.

Having someone from Velia bring up the issue of killing Parmeneides is an extremely elegant idea: just as elegant as the way Plato makes Zeno discredit himself in that other dialogue known as the *Parmenides*. This was one of the wonders of writing fictitious literature. You could create your own reality, make the characters do all the work for you.

But the way Plato uses a term that was so significant for Pythagoreans, and in the mysteries, and above all so relevant to the particular relationship Parmeneides had with Zeno—this is more than simply an accident, and there's more involved here than just a fiction.

Behind the black humour of the joke about patricide there's also some real knowledge about the nature of the relationship between Parmeneides and his successor; only a little knowledge, that's all. Too much familiarity with the facts isn't needed when the aim is to recreate history in line with one's own purposes.

And Plato's purposes are still very clear. Behind everything else, he wanted to be seen as Parmeneides' heir. With any of the other philosophers who lived before him, he really didn't care. But with Parmeneides the situation was different. Plato wanted the succession to his teaching not for Zeno or anyone else, but for himself.

In a sense you could say he succeeded. The fantasy came true. Nowadays there's hardly anyone who doubts that he was Parmeneides' rightful successor: that he took his teaching a stage further, improved it. He succeeded so well that no one really suspects any more how vast the chasm is separating Plato's idea of philosophy from Parmeneides'—or suspects just how much has been left behind.

But in another sense he didn't change a thing. The succession that he wanted to put an end to continued in southern Italy for hundreds of years quite undisturbed, quietly looking back to Parmeneides as its founder, preserving the traces of another reality entirely. And now the discoveries at Velia are like a door left slightly open —giving a glimpse into a landscape that's disconcerting and yet strangely familiar.

For a long time people have puzzled over a mystery that once was described as 'totally incomprehensible'. This is the riddle posed by the complete absence of any connection between Parmeneides, or his philosophy, and the culture they both grew out of: the culture of the Velians and Phocaeans.

In fact the answer to the riddle is very simple. The only lack of connection that exists is between Velian or Phocaean culture and the image of Parmeneides created by Plato.

As for the reality covered over by the image Plato chose to construct, that's quite another matter.

PLATO DIDN'T STOP at creating an alternative reality about the succession to Parmeneides. He also helped do the same thing about Parmeneides' predecessor—and with nearly as much success.

He used to enjoy making jokes about the philosophers who'd lived before him. Humour was one of his most effective weapons in the struggle to establish his own ideas; and he loved presenting genealogies for earlier philosophers that were amusing, striking, frivolous. He didn't even have to invent most of the details. There were entertaining accounts about the origins of philosophy already circulating in ancient Athens.

The one man he mentions in his writings, quite lightheartedly, as Parmeneides' philosophical ancestor was someone called Xenophanes. You could say that linking Parmeneides and Xenophanes had a certain validity: both of them were associated in one way or another with Velia, and there's even a superficial similarity between some of their ideas. But that's all.

And yet what Plato said with his tongue in his cheek quickly came to be accepted as historical fact. His successor Aristotle took on trust, with only a little hesitation, that Xenophanes was Parmeneides' teacher. With Aristotle's own successor the hesitation had already disappeared. It's an old, familiar pattern. Guesses evolve into certainties and dogmas are born.

Soon almost everybody was convinced that the great Parmeneides had been taught what he knew by Xenophanes. But not everybody.

There's one report tucked away in an ancient book written about the lives of the old philosophers that tells a very different story. It briefly notes the standard view about Xenophanes being Parmeneides' teacher—and then goes on to say what's not mentioned in any other surviving source.

It explains that Parmeneides' true teacher wasn't Xenophanes at all because his real connections lay somewhere else entirely.

> He took part in the teaching given by Ameinias the Pythagorean, the son of Diochaitas. Ameinias was a poor man, but a good one and a fine one: this was the man whose teaching he chose to follow. And when Ameinias died he built a hero-shrine for him, belonging as he did to a distinguished and a wealthy family. And it wasn't through Xenophanes but through Ameinias that he was led to stillness (*hêsychia*).

The precision of the details in the report is impressive—so impressive that no one has dared to question its essential accuracy or doubt that it must be based on historical fact. Scholars have been obliged to acknowledge its validity, accept it as authentic.

They've hardly begun to realize what they were taking on board.

Walking Away

T O BEGIN WITH, EVERYTHING WAS ROSES.
The discoveries at Velia were wel-
comed by the learned world with open arms. They were
greeted as 'truly sensational', as calling for a total 'change
of perspective'.

News about them hit the London papers—then it
sank back into silence.

A handful of Italian scholars tried to keep up an
interest in what they all could possibly mean. Otherwise,
people hesitated in the face of the evidence and walked
away. As far as anything to do with Parmeneides was
concerned, their minds were already made up. He was
the father of philosophy, founder of western logic. Long
ago he'd been removed from any contact with life and
made into an abstraction instead, an ideal embodiment
of reason. A few archaeological discoveries were hardly
going to change that.

Looked at from the outside, in terms of ordinary
everyday life, the scholarly reaction seems innocent
enough—even reasonable. But from the inside it's quite
another story.

We honestly believe we're in control, that it's we who search and look and make all the important discoveries in life and know exactly what's important. Occasionally, very occasionally, we may happen to sense something entirely different: that it isn't we who make discoveries at all because really the discoveries draw us to them at the right time and make us find them. It's the discoveries that want to be found and understood.

Just as we like to believe it's we who 'make' discoveries, we also think we 'have' dreams. But what we don't understand is that sometimes beings communicate to us through our dreams, in the same way that they try to communicate through outer events. It can be so difficult for them to draw the attention of the living, to struggle through from their world to this: unimaginably difficult. We have no idea, no inkling, of the particular kind of effort and focus that sometimes is needed.

So we turn away instead.

There were early philosophers—and Parmeneides was one of them—who were quite specific about one point. This is the fact that everything is alive and death is just a name for something we don't understand. It's not an idea of theirs that you often find mentioned. If you take it seriously then it starts to take away too much of the importance of ourselves: raises too many doubts about the reality of what we imagine is reality.

And yet that's one of the first things those early philosophers knew they had to do.

IGNORING SOMETHING needs no justifying when enough people are willing to ignore it. But in the case of the Velian discoveries there was one justification some experts felt able to give for shutting the door before they shut it.

This was to point out what from a distance can seem the one real weakness in the evidence from Velia—the fact that it dates from five hundred years after Parmeneides. Certainly, they said, the details on the inscriptions can be taken to show how people with antiquarian interests at around the time of Christ might have liked to imagine Velia's distant past. But to suppose these details could have any relevance to the period when Parmeneides himself was living: that's 'not correct'.

The reasoning sounds perfectly sensible—provided you don't stop to look at the evidence too long, or too closely.

One of the points in what they said is undeniable. The way the Velian inscriptions were all produced together at the same time shows every trace of antiquarianism, of a self-conscious attempt at celebrating and reviving the memories of days gone by. As a matter of fact the Greeks in southern Italy at that particular time tended to be very glad for any opportunity to parade their past. They'd come to feel so intimidated by the power of Rome that they wanted to prove they, too, had their own claims to fame and glory. It was only natural to want to turn back the clock: to point to traditions that had kept constant through all the centuries of change. It was even natural to clutch at the memory of them years after the life that had created them and then kept them going had gone.

And that's precisely the point. Those people had long memories—a fact that used to be appreciated far more than it is now. The Greeks who'd travelled out to Italy from the east and settled there were notorious in the ancient world for their conservatism, for the way they remembered and honoured and preserved their own past. Even today it's still clear how faithfully they transmitted their religious and magical traditions from one generation to the next, century after century.

Often these traditions were passed on in silence, strictly on a local basis, unknown or almost unknown to anyone outside. A regular time span for the process of transmission was over five hundred years. Sometimes it was closer to a thousand.

This had many implications; but in practice one of the most important things it meant is that evidence dating from a later age often tends to reflect the conditions of a far earlier period. Time and again archaeologists exploring the regions around Velia—towns to the south, or just to the north like Posidonia, or further to the north—discover that religious traditions still being maintained in the first or second centuries AD date all the way back to the sixth and seventh centuries BC.

And throughout the whole of the western Mediterranean there was one particular group of people who had a unique reputation for preserving their original ways and customs. They were more famous than anyone else for their conservatism. They held to the old forms of their language, especially the old Anatolian names, and kept some of the ancient priesthoods alive for nearly a thousand years.

They were the descendants of the Phocaeans who back in the sixth century BC had sailed out to the west. Even at Rome they were considered extraordinary for the way they preserved their ancient traditions, and modern archaeology has helped to show why.

With the new cities they built, the Phocaeans managed to create Anatolias in the west: in Italy and France. And their present was their past.

THE DETAILS ON THE VELIAN INSCRIPTIONS can seem just a jumble of names and figures. It takes a little time spent looking at them for the patterns to emerge.

That Parmeneides' father was called Pyres was hardly a secret in the ancient world. But without the inscriptions nobody would ever have seen quite how significant it is that such a rare name was also known at Miletus. For Miletus didn't only happen to be a major centre in the

Anatolian worship of Apollo Oulios. It was also closely linked with Phocaea in colonizing the Black Sea. And of the two pieces of evidence that throw the clearest light on the Velian title 'Lord of the Lair', one comes from just to the east of Miletus in Caria and the other from a colony founded by Miletus—at Istria on the Black Sea.

There are no coincidences here. The only way that someone in Velia at the time when the inscriptions were made could have managed to preserve this patterning of details was if a continuous tradition had survived for five hundred years. And we can also be more specific.

There's no one who possibly could have remembered those three dates added after the name of each Oulis healer—'in the 280th year', 'in the 379th year', 'in the 446th year'—without the help not just of oral traditions but of something more substantial: written records.

In fact it doesn't need much guessing or searching around to see precisely what kind of records must have been involved. All we have to do is look in the direction indicated by the Velian evidence itself.

Over the last century details have emerged from Miletus about a special group of people. They were dedicated to Apollo. They held enormous political power in the city, as well as religious power; and they were known as the Molpoi.

Names of the individuals involved are carefully listed, one underneath the other, in official inscriptions carved on great blocks of marble. These were people who knew mysteries of Apollo, and transmitted them. Fragments of evidence point to ancient links with heroic 'sons' of Apollo, with ritual piping in his honour—and with the same type of *kouros* traditions once known in Phocaea as well as Crete.

From the late dating of some of the records you might think the whole lineage is only a fantasy. It's not. No more than a few of the marble blocks have been found; but even so, the details of the succession are documented from the early Christian era back to as far as 525 BC.

And things were much the same at Istria—the colony of Miletus on the Black Sea where Apollo was known as Phôleutêrios, the god of lairs and incubation.

There the evidence is even more fragmentary, just as it is at Velia. But we can still see how the family in charge of Apollo's worship survived for seven hundred years.

You'd have to have very good reasons for doubting the historical reality behind the Velian inscriptions, just as you'd have to have good reasons to doubt what they imply: that Parmeneides was someone intimately associated with those Lords of the Lair.

And yet there are none. The only real reasons are reasons to the contrary.

But simply to focus on the inscriptions is to overlook something far more important. This is the way that they agree with the poetry written by Parmeneides himself.

In both cases there's the same fundamental involvement with incubation and dreams and other states of consciousness, with incantations and ecstasy, with Apollo and the underworld. And it's good to remember that—years before the archaeological discoveries were even made—aspects of Parmeneides' poem were already being explained in terms of incubation, shamanism, the practices of Iatromantis figures. The new finds at Velia only help to fill out the background. They bring everything back down to earth.

For thousands of years now, the beginnings of western philosophy have systematically been split off and dissociated from the kind of practices we've come to think of as 'magical'. The process has been a long and determined one; it almost succeeded. But those ancient connections are calling out again to be acknowledged—and it's good to have some sense of the real issues involved.

Talking about how philosophy and magic once were two halves of a whole might sound an interesting historical topic. But basically it's not a matter of history at all. And neither does it mean we just need to be more aware of how irrationality has come to be separated off in our lives from rationality; nor does it even mean we should be making a greater effort to bring everything that seems unreasonable into some harmony with reason. If we think it's enough to do any of that we're still missing the main point, because all these distinctions between rational and irrational are only valid from the limited standpoint of what we call reason.

When rationality is really combined with irrationality, then we begin to go beyond them both. Something else is created, something quite extraordinary that's timeless—and yet entirely new. Then we start seeing the illogicality of everything that normally is considered so reasonable. And we come face to face with an implacable, fascinatingly coherent logic that there can seem a hundred good reasons for dismissing as completely absurd.

This is the logic Parmeneides tried to introduce to the West: a logic that questions everything, that was meant to turn people's lives and values upside down. But we managed to take the easy way out, the reasonable way.

We turned his teaching upside down instead.

IT'S QUITE AN ACHIEVEMENT. We've actually succeeded in creating the illusion that we're wiser than people used to be.

As for those philosopher figures who stand in the distant past at the beginnings of western culture, we've learned to excuse them—to make allowances for the way they failed to draw the conclusions we think they should have drawn.

And yet the only allowances we need to make are for ourselves. We're in no position at all to judge those philosophers: they're our judges. When we close the door on them, we're only closing the door on ourselves.

Those inscriptions found at Velia have their purpose and their message. Walking away from them might seem very easy. But it isn't easy at all, because nothing exists in isolation.

If you dismiss them you have to dismiss their whole Anatolian background; then you have to deny their links with Parmeneides' poem. And even that's only the beginning. For they're also linked up with a whole network of other traditions about Parmeneides and the people close to him, traditions that have been known about but covered over for ages.

Everything is stitched up together. It's all of a piece. And our past is stitched up in it too—along with our future.

Ameinias

P ARMENEIDES' TEACHER, AMEINIAS, WAS A
poor man.

Probably you'd have noticed nothing special about
him at all if you passed him in the street. Outwardly
there'd have been very little to set him apart from anyone
else.

With Parmeneides himself it was a different matter.
In the report about his teacher he's presented as someone who belonged to a distinguished and wealthy family.
And we're told in a rather obscure way that this explains
why he built the hero-shrine for Ameinias.

The connection between coming from a family
that's eminent as well as rich and building someone a
shrine seems reasonable enough. But it isn't completely
obvious. There have even been scholars who felt the
connection is so artificial that the Greek text of the report
must be wrong; that somehow it needs correcting. And
yet we're already in a position to start understanding why
the report says what it says.

Anatolian families of priests in the service of Apollo
the healer used to be outstandingly distinguished as well

as rich; and they happened to demonstrate these qualities most tangibly in one particular way.

That was through the remarkable size and extraordinary workmanship of the shrines, tombs and monuments they used to build. This is plainest of all in traditions emanating from Miletus. But it's especially clear in the evidence from Miletus' colony at Istria—the same town where Apollo was worshipped as the god in charge of lairs, Phôleutêrios.

So the circle completes itself again. The background to the report about Parmeneides and Ameinias agrees exactly with the background to the series of inscriptions from Velia: Parmeneides as a priest of Apollo the healer, the Anatolian god of incubation.

A HERO-SHRINE was something quite exceptional.

In Parmeneides' own time, building one for someone who'd died was extremely unusual—regardless of how rich or poor you were. As a rule people were buried with a simple ritual. Building a hero-shrine was another matter entirely.

And it meant certain things. It involved creating a special hero-cult: meant marking off a precinct for the worship of someone who was considered more than the human being he or she had appeared to be.

Basically, to be treated as a hero was to be treated as a mythical being. It was the equivalent of being seen as belonging to another world, another race, another time. Deep inside us we've all had a glimpse of that world and that time at one moment or another. But to live what we've glimpsed, or allow it to be lived—that's something else.

And none of this ever happened without a proper reason, without a justification to give it sense. For there was always something extraordinary about heroes, just as there was about the creation of hero-shrines.

That makes it all the stranger how nobody has noted one very simple detail: the way that Ameinias being worshipped as a hero after he died is paralleled by the tradition of Oulis healers treating Parmeneides himself as a hero. In terms of understanding Parmeneides the parallel speaks volumes. You could say it means that heroes don't simply appear out of nowhere; that sometimes it takes a hero to make a hero.

The whole saga of the Phocaeans' journey to the west and the origins of Velia had been a story about Apollo and oracles, riddles and heroes. It had all happened such a short time before.

And now Parmeneides was continuing the tradition.

THE REPORT ABOUT AMEINIAS describes him as a Pythagorean.

Like everything else in the report, the detail is significant. You only have to glance at the evidence that survives to notice how the whole question of heroes—their status, their true identity, the right attitude to adopt towards them, how to become one—played a crucial part in early Pythagorean tradition.

But this isn't to say we should lose sight of the fact that heroes along with hero-shrines were among the most fundamental aspects of ancient Greek religion. And they weren't anything to do with commemorating the dead, with trying to honour the past or keep old memories alive.

They had to do with something entirely different.

Hero-shrines were all about presence, living presence. They were about maintaining a correct relationship with the power the hero had become, and they were meant to create the circumstances that would allow this power to be as effective as possible in the present. The existence of a hero-shrine was supposed to be a blessing for the whole area: for the land and the local people, for nature and for visitors.

There was nothing casual about creating a hero-shrine—or about making it a part of your life. It was an opening to another world. If you went near one you had to pass it in total silence. And for Greeks in general, but especially for the Pythagoreans, silence and stillness went hand in hand. They were two aspects of the same thing.

This is why *hêsychia*, the Greek word that means 'stillness', automatically included the meaning 'silence' as well. But according to the report about Ameinias, *hêsychia* is precisely the quality that Parmeneides was expressing his gratitude to him for when he built the hero-shrine. It was the quality Ameinias had brought into his life— or rather had brought him towards.

You can already see from this how the details in the report wrap around each other, fit together, how there's nothing random or arbitrary about them at all. Even if you were reading a work of fiction you'd be likely to notice them, realize they're significant.

But this isn't just fiction. It happened.

AND THERE'S MORE to hero-shrines than that.

Because heroes had been humans but also were more than humans, it was understood that they had a special relationship with what lies beyond the limits of ordinary human experience—with the world of the dead, the underworld.

They had power over health and sickness and death. If you approached them the right way they could heal you. Or they'd show their presence and guidance instead in your ordinary, daily life through special signs and uncanny coincidences: by communicating through outer events.

But there's one method of communication that they preferred to any other. This was through people's dreams.

If you look back you can see the extraordinary consistency—and simplicity—in the way early Christianity converted the places that once had been hero-shrines into shrines for saints. There was hardly anything anyone had to do except change the names. And the one most fundamental feature that the Christian worship of saints took over from the Greek worship of heroes was the practice of incubation. Incubation for Greeks was such an essential aspect of communicating with heroes, was accepted so naturally as the normal thing to do at hero-shrines, that most ancient writers just took this for granted. The only thing they felt might ever need some explaining was the very occasional exception: the extraordinary case where apparently a hero-shrine had nothing at all to do with dreams or incubation.

The link between hero-shrines and incubation was so close that wherever incubation was practised, heroes usually weren't too far away. Most often incubation centres simply were centres for the worship of heroes. But even in other cases the link is still clear—even from passages like the one Strabo wrote about the cave at

Acharaca in Caria and about the shrine just below it that was sacred to Persephone and Hades.

First of all he mentions the shrine and the cave and the mysteries, practised there in utter silence; and then he goes on to say there was another cave not far away where the local people also used to go. It was across the nearby mountain, beside a beautiful meadow known as 'Asia'.

According to tradition this cave was connected underground with the other cave at Acharaca. It was sacred to the same gods too, because here was the legendary site where Hades had married Persephone— the original place where he'd snatched her down into the underworld.

And the monument that marked the spot was a hero-shrine.

THEN THERE'S THE MOST IMPORTANT PART of the report as far as Parmeneides' relationship with his teacher is concerned. This is the statement that it was Ameinias who 'led him to stillness', to *hêsychia*.

Scholars have translated the statement quite effortlessly. They say it means Ameinias converted Parmencides to the philosophical life, to the contemplative life, 'the quiet life'.

And yet these are just interpretations, not translations. As for the idea of one philosopher leading or urging another on towards his teaching, this is a theme that became familiar enough in the ancient world. It's also true that the question of stillness eventually became a significant topic, in some Greek philosophical circles, as a result of direct contact with India. But that doesn't explain the mention here of stillness with such specific reference to Parmeneides; and there's nothing at all to be gained from converting such a particular detail into some commonplace.

There are a number of things about the word *hêsychia* that are well worth noting. You could mention its close connections with healing—or the fact that it was a quality often associated with one particular god, Apollo. But that's not what's most crucial.

Ameinias is presented as a Pythagorean; and the Pythagoreans happened to attach extraordinary importance to stillness. This wasn't just a matter of the silence imposed on people who wanted to become Pythagoreans. That was a part of the picture, but only a small part. For behind the silence there was a whole dimension of significance to the practice of stillness.

It all had to do with dreams, with other states of awareness. The outer techniques of stillness that Pythagoreans practised—the silence, the deliberate calm, physically not even moving—weren't simply ends in themselves. They were means that were used for the sake of reaching something else.

And their purpose was straightforward enough, even though the ancient sources speak a language most of us no longer understand or want to understand.

The purpose was to free people's attention from distractions, to turn it in another direction so their awareness could start operating in an entirely different way. The stillness had a point to it, and that was to create an opening into a world unlike anything we're used to: a world that can only be entered 'in deep meditation, ecstasies and dreams'.

What Ameinias taught Parmeneides wasn't anything to do with thinking as we understand thinking, or philosophical reflection. It had to do with incubation. The decisive characteristic of the tradition kept going for hundreds of years by those men called Phôlarchos— by Lords of the Lair who traced their origin back to Parmeneides—also turns out to be the defining characteristic of what Parmeneides himself received from his teacher.

And even the Greek language makes the link between them and what he learned from Ameinias quite clear. For *hêsychia* and *phôleos* are two words that happen to belong together: repeatedly they occur side by side in ancient Greek. When Strabo tried to describe what happened at the incubation shrine near Acharaca he wasn't the only writer who chose to sum up the experience of lying motionless—just like an animal in a *phôleos* or lair—by using the word *hêsychia*.

PARMENEIDES' PREDECESSOR and his successors are united by one common factor. That's stillness, the stillness experienced in incubation. This is what defined their basic focus, their mode of operation.

To suppose that Parmeneides himself—disciple of Ameinias, exemplar of the Oulis healers—could have been exempt from this same concern would be totally illogical. And in fact we haven't even started to see what a central place he gave to stillness, or *hêsychia*, in his teaching as a whole.

But behind these details about Parmeneides and the people who once were close to him there's the question of what they all mean: of how to understand what the details point to.

The question couldn't be a more basic one. For the connecting thread of stillness linking Parmeneides to the people who came before and after him is obvious enough when you care to look—and yet it's no accident that no one has recognized or noticed it.

The fact is that these things have an uncanny way of protecting themselves. And even what at one moment might seem obvious in the next moment isn't obvious at all. This is exactly what happens when you engage with a reality that, just like the reality of heroes, belongs to another world.

Like the Wind at Night

W E ALL KNOW WHAT STILLNESS IS; OR AT LEAST WE think we do.

It means peace and pleasantness, lying under the sun for half an hour with the thoughts racing through our minds about what to do later in the day.

And if we're honest, we'll probably have to admit that the statement about Parmeneides being led by Ameinias to stillness sounds ridiculous. If it was a matter of the great Parmeneides being taught lofty truths about the universe and metaphysics and the nature of man and woman, this wouldn't be a problem. But to be told that the one thing he learned from his teacher was stillness— that's an absurd anticlimax.

The absurdity is a warning: an accurate sign of just how hopeless it is to try fitting Parmeneides, or the world he used to move in, into our normal frame of reference. As to how serious we are about heeding the warning, that's another matter.

FOR THE GREEKS, stillness had a whole side to it that they found intensely disquieting—and not just disquieting but also sinister, alien, profoundly inhuman.

That's why they associated stillness and silence so closely with the process of approaching heroes. And it's also why that little report about Ameinias isn't the only ancient text to bring the two subjects of stillness and heroes together, to set them side by side.

A strange piece of writing was produced during the centuries after Parmeneides. It's called the *Pythagorean Memoirs*. To read it you have to be on your guard: the style of presentation seems so casual and smooth that you can easily miss the sequence of ideas, not notice all the threads holding them in place. And at first sight you could think it's pure chance that one passage in the *Memoirs* mentions the two themes of heroes and stillness together—referring now to stillness, now to heroes, and then back again to stillness and to heroes.

In fact this has nothing to do with chance. It's stillness that has the power to carry a human being into another reality: into a world of prophecy where future and past and present are all contained and where heroes, not humans, are at home.

But stillness wasn't associated only with heroes. Beyond even the heroes were the gods; and when Greeks wanted to describe in tangible terms the reality of a confrontation between humans and the divine, there was one particular quality that they sensed as characterizing the gods in contrast to people.

This was their uncanny stillness. Gods stayed totally calm when humans would panic. They wouldn't even change their expression when people ran through the whole range of emotions from joy to terror. They'd stay exactly the same: enigmatic. Even the most dramatic miracles or displays of power weren't as effective a way of emphasizing the difference between humans and gods as the utter unshakability of divine stillness.

That's the real reason for the stillness practised in incubation. It was a method for coming as close as possible to the divine world. And this is why according to the normal terms of Greek religion incubation was strictly limited to special, sacred places—to territory where gods and heroes, not humans, were in charge. For the stillness itself was something that belonged to the heroes and the gods.

From a certain perspective it's true enough to say that the stillness of incubation was simply a technique, a means to an end, a way of contacting the divine. And yet that's only how it seems to us.

Really it was already the end itself, the ultimate paradox of the end that's present at the beginning.

AT ONE POINT the writer of those *Pythagorean Memoirs* makes a statement that can sound extraordinary. He says that stillness is simply impossible for human beings. Men and women can try to be good—and they can even succeed. But stillness is something beyond their power.

And yet this isn't such an extraordinary point to make, especially for a Pythagorean. In the writings left behind by people known as Pythagoreans certain things are considered basic facts of life. One of them is that as humans we're always changing, restless. At every moment our bodies are moving—and not just our bodies but our thoughts and desires as well. Anybody who was able to maintain a visibly greater degree of stillness than people in general was assumed to be divine: considered someone who's more than human, who belongs to another world.

Now it should be possible to see why Parmeneides needed someone very special and very powerful to lead him to stillness. And it should also be clear exactly why he built that shrine for Ameinias—why he established the worship of him as a being who was mysterious, divine.

He created the hero-shrine because the stillness he'd been brought to was itself something mysterious and divine. It wasn't human at all.

AND YET at the same time there's nothing more human than that stillness.

Life for us has become an endless affair of trying to improve ourselves: achieving more and doing more, learning more, always needing to know more things. The process of learning and being taught has simply become a matter of being fed facts and information—receiving what we didn't have before, always being given something different from ourselves.

That's why whatever we learn never touches us deeply enough, why nothing really satisfies us. And the more we sense this the more we rush around trying to find other substitutes to fill the void we still feel inside. Everything pushes us outside ourselves—further away from the utter simplicity of our own humanity.

It's quite true that the Pythagoreans had their teachings, too. But there's also something about the Pythagorean tradition that's completely different from all this, like an undercurrent moving in exactly the opposite direction. It's something that's hardly ever noticed or mentioned, for the simple reason that it doesn't seem to make any sense.

Pythagoreans were famous not just for their teachings but also for the secrecy of their teachings. And yet when you start to look closely at what have come to be considered the most esoteric of their doctrines, it turns out that really they weren't secret at all. In fact they were little more than window-dressing. They served a very valuable purpose: they aroused general interest, helped attract the people who eventually might become Pythagoreans.

But once someone became a Pythagorean, it started to become a matter of learning less and less. There were fewer answers, and more riddles. Techniques could be provided for entering other states of consciousness. Otherwise, the emphasis was placed less and less on being given teachings and more and more on finding the inner resources to discover your own answers inside yourself.

This is why teaching through riddles was such an important part of Pythagorean tradition. Instead of being fed with ready-made answers you were just given the germ, the seed, of the answer: for the riddle contains its own solution.

Your job was to feed the riddle, nurture it. And it was understood that, through the process of being tended and attended to, the riddle would become an organic part of yourself. As it grew it had the power to transform you. It could even destroy you. But the aim of the riddle was as clear as it was subtle—to shift the focus of attention away from superficial answers towards discovering what you hadn't realized you're already carrying around inside yourself.

You can see the same basic situation in the case of that man from Posidonia who helped the Phocaeans when they were totally lost. The Phocaeans had their oracle from Apollo, together with the guidance it contained. But in spite of that, or rather because of that, everything had become hopeless for them. It wasn't just that the oracle had become a meaningless riddle. Their whole existence had become one living riddle.

In a sense you could say that the man from Posidonia gave them something: that he provided them with the answer they hadn't noticed. But that's only true on a very superficial level. Really he didn't add anything essential to their situation at all. He was just there, in the right place and at the right time, to point to the solution already contained inside the riddle they were carrying with them—the riddle they'd become.

AND IT WAS THE SAME with Ameinias, as well.

Everything had been laid out for Parmeneides. As an Ouliadês he occupied his place in a tradition reaching back to the days when the Phocaeans hadn't yet left Anatolia: a tradition based on techniques of stillness and incubation.

So the obvious question is how Ameinias could possibly fit in. And there's a very simple answer. He doesn't.

Logically you would think that Parmeneides didn't have any need for anybody's teaching, least of all the teaching of a nobody like Ameinias. But that's to forget one fundamental thing. The knowledge we already have is useless unless we can really live it, in and through ourselves. Otherwise it becomes a burden that can weigh us down or even destroy us, like the oracle of the Phocaeans.

We already have everything we need. We just need to be shown what we have. And it's the same with traditions. Even the strongest of them have to be revitalized, because it's so easy for them to become weighed down as well. The life in them can die out without anyone even noticing, or wanting to notice. And usually it's a complete outsider, a nobody—someone who doesn't fit in, who logically is quite unnecessary—who has to inject the life that's needed.

This is why the greatest teachers are often utter nobodies. They're nobodies who give nothing at all. But that nothing is worth more than everything else. In some circumstances they might introduce you to a new system of knowledge, or demand that you change your lifestyle —and yet that's not what the teaching is basically about. It's just a trick to keep your mind focused while the real work is done on another level, somewhere else.

Real teachers leave no traces. They're like the wind at night rushing right through you and totally changing you but leaving everything unchanged, even your greatest weaknesses; blowing away every idea of what you thought you were and leaving you as you always have been, since the beginning.

FOUR

Playing with Toys

F EBRUARY 29, 1968.
'Assolutamente sicura'—it's absolutely certain. There's no doubt about it. It was there all along, just where you'd expect to find it.

I've found his head! You don't have to believe me. Anyone can see how perfectly it fits; every crack, every trace confirms it.

And of course people did doubt, needlessly. For everything Mario Napoli wrote in his letter to a famous art historian from Switzerland was quite true. After nearly two thousand years—and after summer after summer of patiently sifting the Italian soil—the head of Parmeneides had at last been reunited with its base.

But, as always, there was an irony to the situation.

You'd find it very natural to assume that the face on the sculpture must be the face of the man whose name is spelled out on the inscription at the base.

It's not. The delicate eyes and nose and hair carved in the fine white marble are simply standard, stereotyped features. They don't show Parmeneides at all. When the sculpture was created, at around the time of Christ, people had completely forgotten what he looked like.

AND MUCH MORE had been forgotten than just faces.

The way all those inscriptions for Parmeneides and the Oulis healers, along with the matching sculptures, were produced together at the same time is more reminiscent of a portrait gallery or waxwork museum than of anything else. Clearly they were parts of one great systematic project aimed at commemorating an ancient Velian tradition. But the problem is that when you try to commemorate the past and keep it alive like this, that's when the past is already dead.

It's no wonder that so soon—only a few years after they'd been created—those memorials had been broken up, turned upside down, walked all over and buried. The details preserved on the inscriptions were impeccably correct and self-consistent; but the essence of the tradition that the memorials represented, the living reality, had gone.

Times had changed. In the West the focus of interest had started shifting to other things instead. The love of wisdom had been replaced by philosophy, been made appealing and accessible to the curious mind. And what once demanded everything you are was gradually being turned into a pastime for people who love playing with toys.

Parmeneides' own teaching had been torn away from the background and context that had given it its meaning and life. What originally had been intended to involve every fibre of one's being was converted into a dry logic that's only good for complicating and torturing our minds. Now we don't even remember what happened, and we're no longer able to tell the difference.

This all served its purpose—the way things always do. And there's no right, or wrong. People just do what's needed at the time. You could say that Plato and Aristotle, in particular, simply did their job: they made it possible for us to develop our intelligence in certain directions, to explore aspects of ourselves that we hadn't known before. But then the time comes to be moving on.

And yet before that can happen we first have to see what brought us to where we are. For history isn't really the facts and figures we read about in textbooks; and the versions of the past that we're so used to are like veils and coverings, hiding far more than they reveal.

OFTEN IT'S SAID how much we owe to ancient Athens. This is true—but not in quite the way we've been led to believe.

Athens used to be a major centre of culture in the Mediterranean. It was only one of them; there were others, too. But it became an important centre for people who were so clever and ambitious that they led the West to believe it owes almost everything to them. We still believe them, and histories of the ancient world are still based on Athenian propaganda.

It was people at Athens who invented the fiction of a united Greece. But really there never was a united Greece, because so many Greeks wanted very little to do with Athens. A few talented Athenians perfected a bizarre game called 'democracy'. They offered other Greek states and cities the opportunity to play—in return for their submission. If they refused to accept, they destroyed them. Many Greek centres of culture preferred to side with the Persians rather than with Athens. They considered them more civilized.

And there were Greeks who, as one historian wrote, found themselves in the position of deciding 'to contribute to destroying once and for all what remained of the Athenians'. Those people had a very different story to tell from the one we've become accustomed to. It's a strange story, preserved here and there as small fragments in ancient texts or as scraps of information hidden away in the most unlikely of places where hardly anyone cares to look.

And it's strange not only because of what happened, but because of the need we still feel to believe things happened otherwise.

AT LEAST on the surface, some Greeks seemed more moderate and diplomatic in their attitude to Athens.

There's one small statement about a well-known citizen of Velia: Parmeneides' successor, Zeno. It's hardly the most dramatic thing to be told. All it says is that

> he had a greater love for his home town—a plain, worthless kind of place that was only good at producing fine men—than for the arrogance of the Athenians. So he didn't often visit Athens but passed his life at home.

We in the West have become so totally, and unconsciously, identified with Athens that the most natural way to make sense of such a blatant affront is to explain it away: to say that the statement was obviously invented by some writer with a personal grudge, a little axe to grind. And yet there's much more involved here than one person's grudge.

The contrast between the grand city of Athens and Velia with its simplicity and plainness sounds so neat that you might suppose it's nothing but a nice rhetorical touch, devoid of any historical value. You'd be wrong, because there's more to the contrast than that.

In fact Velia was built exactly the same way as its sister city at Marseilles, or Phocaea itself—on a patch of land beside the sea that was so barren and worthless hardly any other Greeks would have dreamed of creating their home there. The ruggedness of all three settlements, the poverty of the land, were self-evident facts to anyone who knew about the places. And even today you can still see from the ruins just how fond the Phocaeans were of keeping to basics; of building their towns in harsh places, paradigms of plainness and austerity.

As for the remark about Zeno's attitude to Athens: in its own simple, quiet way it strikes right at the heart of the treasured assumption that Athens was the be-all and end-all of the ancient world. But what's even more informative than the statement itself is how it's come to be treated—the ways people have found of discrediting it, dismissing it, disposing of it.

Scholars have insisted, for one thing, on changing the Greek text. And there are those who mistranslate the passage, as well. In place of any reference to 'the arrogance of the Athenians' they make it say that Zeno preferred his home town 'to the magnificence of Athens', or 'before all the splendour of Athens': a little indication of how deep the allegiance to Athens still goes.

Then there's that matter of altering the original text. It's a peculiar affair. The Greek manuscripts clearly say that Zeno 'didn't often visit Athens'; but over a hundred years ago one editor decided to change the text here and make them say 'he never visited Athens' instead. Everyone who's ever translated the passage or commented on it since then has accepted the change without question.

And yet there was no real reason to alter the text at all—except that the change has one remarkably devious advantage.

If the passage is made to say that Zeno never went to Athens, then it plainly contradicts the picture Plato presents in his *Parmenides* of Zeno visiting Athens together with his teacher. And considering the immense authority Plato has managed to win as a respectable source of information about the ancient world, the contradiction proves just as plainly that the whole passage about Zeno and his dislike for the Athenians is a deliberate forgery.

But of course there's no contradiction, apart from the one that's been invented. And yet to say this isn't quite the end of the matter.

For in the case of that picture Plato presented of Parmeneides and Zeno at Athens, there's rather more involved than meets the eye.

WHEN PLATO WROTE his *Parmenides* he knew he was writing first-class historical make-believe: putting imaginary dialogue, brilliantly lifelike, into the mouths of real people who'd lived about a hundred years before him.

And he wasn't the only writer in his own time who was an expert at creating precisely this type of intricate fictional dialogue. But even he could hardly have imagined just how seriously people in later generations would take the things he wrote.

With the help of Platonists, especially, the fictions in his *Parmenides* and other dialogues snowballed. Soon everyone knew the names of the Athenians Zeno had taught—and exactly what he'd taught them. People started expounding the profound symbolism of the *Parmenides*, as well: of how philosophers had had to travel all the way to Athens so that their teachings could be analyzed, corrected, given their ultimate form by Socrates and Plato.

But there's another sense too, a very different one, in which the dialogue is symbolic.

If you look closely at the picture Plato painted, cracks start to appear. And if—as a couple of scholars have done—you look through the cracks you begin to glimpse quite another scene behind. For there's evidence that does suggest Parmeneides and Zeno did come to Athens, not to have some theoretical conversation about Plato's ideas but in a legal and political capacity: as ambassadors from Velia, as negotiators of peace.

And the evidence that there is suggests they didn't come to ask the Athenians for help, or support, but that their purpose was to do what they could to prevent Athens from interfering with the delicate balance of power in southern Italy. Their main aim in visiting the city wasn't to chat about philosophy. It was much more practical—far more practical than we might guess.

The Lawgivers

'HE GAVE LAWS TO THE CITIZENS.'
Several writers in the ancient world said this about Parmeneides. Some of them also mentioned that each year the leaders of Velia used to make the citizens swear they'd stay true to his original laws—and that Zeno, in turn, had been responsible for governing the city.

One of these writers was Plato's nephew. There were few people in a position to know better. He'd travelled out westwards together with Plato, and had managed to gain more direct access to information about political or legal history in southern Italy and Sicily than almost any other writer we know of.

This isn't exactly the most predictable thing to be told about Parmeneides, or about Zeno. But, there again, not a great deal about either of them is particularly predictable. Most historians haven't had the faintest idea what to make of it. And if pressed, as a rule they'll tend to say it can't have any real significance because it has no bearing at all on Parmeneides' philosophy: on the teachings in his poem.

Nothing could possibly be further from the truth. It's quite amazing to watch how scholars are so occupied with squeezing an abstract, theoretical sense out of Parmeneides' poetry that they manage not to notice one very simple fact. The central, most important part of his poem is formally presented as the record of a legal process, phrased in standard legal terminology.

And already this neglected fact allows a glimpse into an ancient, secret drama. Moses brought his laws down from Mount Sinai; Parmeneides brought his back from the depths of hell.

To UNDERSTAND SOMETHING, you always have to have somewhere to start. We have somewhere to start.

Parmeneides was an Ouliadês who was intimately involved with the service of Apollo; and Apollo had the strongest and closest of ties with lawgiving.

You can see a particularly fine example of this at Miletus—the famous old Carian city where that group of people known as the Molpoi used to live.

The Molpoi weren't just responsible for transmitting mysteries of Apollo, or ancient *kouros* traditions, from century to century. They were also lawgivers for the city. Inside Miletus itself they were in charge of domestic legal matters. And in relation to other cities they had another role that was very plainly defined. They acted formally as ambassadors: as negotiators of peace.

But it's not just a question of links between Apollo and lawgiving—although these are certainly important enough. For ourselves, we tend to be happiest treating things in isolation. And yet the Greeks weren't quite like that, as so much of the evidence still shows.

There used to be a great philosopher who lived in Sicily. He was deeply influenced by Pythagoreans, and by Parmeneides in particular. He also happens to have been not only a magician but a Iatromantis as well: a 'healer–prophet', a healer who works through prophecy.

He wrote poetry, like Parmeneides. And in his poetry he mentions a tradition that eventually was carried down to Egypt as Pythagoreans started leaving Italy and Sicily for the great new city called Alexandria. According to this tradition, there are four basic vocations that can give human beings a special degree of closeness to the divine. The vocations are prophet, poet, healer, and political leader or lawgiver.

These might sound a random enough collection to us. But in fact every one of them is connected to every other. And the clearest sign of their connectedness is the fact that they're all activities sacred to the same god: Apollo.

In the case of the philosopher and Iatromantis from Sicily, people have noticed for a long time that when he describes the four vocations he's actually describing himself. He lived them all.

But now we're in a position where we can start to see that he wasn't the only person who embodied each of these roles in himself. From the discoveries at Velia—together with what remains of Parmeneides' poem, as well as the other traditions about him—it's already becoming clear that the same was true of the man he admired and was influenced by so much.

This isn't simply a matter of biography, of interesting details from Parmeneides' life. In fact it's only when we notice how the roles of Iatromantis and of lawgiver influenced even the smallest aspects of his poetry that we can really begin to understand what he was saying.

ONCE AGAIN we have to turn to Plato—and to the last work he ever wrote. It's called *The Laws*.

Right at the heart of the whole work there's the image of an ideal city. And right at the heart of the city, the key to its existence, is its governing body.

Plato was perfectly clear about the main details of how it's to be governed. The highest authorities in preserving justice and supervising matters of law are to be priests but not just any kind of priests. Quite specifically, they're to be joint priests 'of Apollo and the Sun'.

He went on to explain at great length how, after these people die, they're to be treated and worshipped as heroes. And the overall features of what he describes—the lives of the priests, their deaths—aren't his invention at all. It was shown some time ago that they derive from what he learned about at first hand on his visits to southern Italy and Sicily: in fact they faithfully reflect Pythagorean traditions and practices.

Really there's no need to be surprised at finding Pythagorean traditions being given such a central place in his final work. Pythagoreans governed whole cities in southern Italy according to their own principles. They managed to bring together the inner and outer, politics and the love of wisdom, theory and practice, in a way Plato himself was never able to imitate or achieve. Ever since his visit to them while he was still fairly young he'd borrowed so much from them—especially his myths and mythical images.

And it was there, among the Pythagoreans, that even towards the end of his days he saw his own unrealized ideal of the philosopher who's also a lawgiver actually lived out and fulfilled.

MORE THAN ONCE IN HIS LIFETIME Plato stated in no uncertain terms that the final, ultimate authority for a true lawgiver has to be Apollo. 'If we know what we're doing' then Apollo is the god to whom the most fundamental matters of law will be entrusted.

And he was careful to include—among the most important and essential of all these matters of law—one particular issue that by now should be very familiar. This is the issue of the exact procedures to be followed by a lawgiver in building hero-shrines and establishing the worship of heroes.

But Plato was also careful to explain as precisely as possible just what's expected of the lawgivers in such cases, to specify their role and function. And they're not quite what you'd expect.

One of the most crucial things they have to do is this: simply to follow the guidance that's been given to people 'through divine visions, or else through inspiration received by someone from the gods and then disclosed to others'. So for all their high position, for all the influence and power you'd imagine they would have, the lawgivers aren't supposed to take the initiative at all in matters of the greatest importance or do things in the way that they themselves might like. They're not even allowed to.

Their job is to follow and accept, take note and obey. Essentially they just have to let themselves be guided by the inspirations or visions once given to others, resisting any temptation to interfere. 'In all these things the lawgiver mustn't change even the smallest detail.'

And there's not the slightest doubt about the kind of practice Plato had in mind. For in fact he's referring to something very specific.

Legends still survive about the greatest of the ancient lawgivers in southern Italy—lawgivers who happen to have been seen as particularly important figures by Pythagoreans. In social terms they might have been nobodies, the poorest of the poor. But this didn't prevent them being taken seriously, or being treated with every possible honour, when they disclosed to others what today would be unthinkable: that gods had come to them in a dream and given them laws.

We still know quite a few names of Greeks—and non-Greeks—who once were famous for having laws revealed to them in visions or dreams. You can find them listed in modern books alongside Parmeneides because, just as he described at the start of his poem how he'd received his knowledge of reality by meeting a goddess, they were said to have received their laws through encounters with a goddess or god.

But there's one thing that hasn't been noticed in the process of drawing up these lists. Parmeneides' own reputation among the Greeks wasn't only for being an inspired philosopher or poet. He was also known as a lawgiver himself.

And if we look, we can start to see the reasons why.

AT THE END OF HIS *LAWS*, in the very last lines and words he ever published, Plato added one extra dimension to his image of an ideal city.

Since then, it's been a cause of endless confusion. Historians have offered the most extraordinary explanations for it; others dismiss it as completely superfluous, redundant, a sign of growing senility.

He described how behind the governing body with the greatest apparent authority in matters of law there's to be another even more powerful group of people, also made up to a large extent of those priests of Apollo and the Sun. This will be a group responsible not just for making or supervising laws but for continually deepening its understanding of their purpose, their source.

And what's strangest of all about this group of people is the name he decided to give it—as well as the time he specified for when they need to meet.

He called it the Night Gathering; and in spite of the name he insisted that it has to assemble every single day not at the beginning or middle of the night but during the precise interval 'from earliest dawn until sunrise'.

Certainly he gave a reason for why it has to meet then, rather than at any other time: 'because this is the time that will allow everyone involved the greatest leisure and freedom from their other activities and commitments'.

But whatever else most scholars have felt about Plato's idea of a Night Gathering, they haven't been able to help suspecting that this talk of schedules and free time is just a trivialization—a weak rationalizing of something else.

They're quite right. To understand what's involved you only have to remember the Pythagoreans in southern Italy, and their appreciation for the lesson Orpheus learned when he went down through incubation to the world of the dead: that Apollo is fundamentally linked to Night because both their powers have one and the same source.

But that's not all. There's also the oldest known account of Orpheus' descent to the underworld, which happens as well to be the oldest known passage identifying the Sun with Apollo. The passage describes what Orpheus—priest of Apollo and the Sun—used to do after he'd gone down to the underworld and seen what there is to be seen there. It explains how 'he would get up at night', while people were still asleep, climb a mountain, and 'wait from earliest dawn until sunrise so he could be the first to catch a glimpse of the Sun'.

And what he saw when the sun rose wasn't just the object we see in the sky, but what he'd been shown in another world.

Always Plato is praised for his extraordinary creativity as a writer; for the wonderfully evocative quality of his myths and mythical imagery. What's never noticed is the ways he chose to take over older mythological traditions and—through lack of interest, or simply as a result of misunderstanding—obscure their significance, jumble the details, blur the edges of what once had been the finest of distinctions. What's never even mentioned is just how much was covered over and lost.

AND YOU MIGHT ASK: is the fact that Orpheus was a priest of Apollo and the Sun the only reason why the mythology about him had such a particular influence in shaping what Plato talked about right at the end of his book on laws? Or could it be that somewhere there's more to the matter than this?

The answer is that there is.

Those south-Italian vases that show Orpheus while he's in the underworld also show him together with the goddess Justice. When he comes face to face with Persephone, Justice is standing in the background. And there are passages from Orphic poetry that fill in a few of the gaps about this shadowy figure.

The name of her father was Law. And apart from her we're told that there was another goddess who also kept watch beside her, right at the entrance to the cave of Night. While Justice has the job of making sure that laws are respected and justice is done, this other goddess is the maker and creator of laws. She's the divine lawgiver for the universe.

So when Parmeneides went down to the under-world, to the realms of Night and the goddess Justice, he was taken to precisely the place where all laws come from: to the mythical source of lawgiving where the lawgiver is given his laws.

PARMENEIDES' GODDESS Justice is simply a philosophical abstraction for scholars nowadays—a symbol for the rigour and correctness of his reasoning powers. But she has a greater significance than that. And it's not just a question of isolated features in some legends about Orpheus.

You may remember about that man from Crete who was called a *kouros*: who was said to have slept in a cave for years and then, when he became famous, explained that his teacher had been his dream.

He's the man who was supposed to have learned about the world of the dead and the judgement of the dead; to have had 'encounters while dreaming with gods and the teachings of gods, and with Justice and Truth'. We've already seen how relevant this is to Parmeneides' own account of his descent into the underworld, of what he learned there about Justice and Truth—and of his meetings with goddesses including Justice herself, guarding the entrance to the Mansions of Night.

But there's even more to these mythical details than you might guess.

According to legend, it was after his encounter with Justice and Truth that the man from Crete was called to ancient Athens to heal the city of a massive plague. And the old stories about him—his name is Epimenides—give a good idea of what form this healing took.

Partly it took the form of rituals demanding patience: involving the ability to watch animals, to follow them in their movements. Partly it was a matter of insisting that Athenians start putting an end to the barbaric subordination of women and treating them less harshly.

But above all, Epimenides' healing of the Athenians was explained as a matter of introducing 'justice' to the city by paving the way for new legislation and laws. This isn't some arbitrary idea. On the contrary, here you can see how deep the connection went for a Iatromantis between healing and lawgiving: to give good laws to a city is to heal it.

And as for the underlying logic and implication in this whole sequence of events, they should be obvious enough. The goddess Justice opens the way to justice. It's through encountering Justice in another world, another state of consciousness, that you're able to bring justice into this.

YOU COULD SAY all this talk about justice and lawgiving and another world is nothing but legends, images, mythology—the stuff that dreams are made of. And you'd have every reason to say so.

But you'd be wrong.

There are other traditions that show Epimenides wasn't the only person from Crete who was known for finding justice as the result of a dream. And even more importantly, they make it clear that Epimenides' legendary experience of happening to fall asleep in a Cretan cave doesn't simply refer to some accident or chance.

For according to these traditions the great lawgivers of Crete were *kouros* figures who had their laws revealed to them, in a cave, through the ritual practice of incubation.

The myths aren't only myths. They point to the actual use of incubatory techniques as a preparation for lawgiving. And they provide a perfect example of what later Greek writers meant when they said incubation had given humans two of the greatest blessings—healing, and good laws.

So we're brought back to incubation once again. Again, behind the veil of abstractions that we've come to insist is all that exists we're faced with the traces of another reality: a reality once entered and experienced by people who knew how.

And as far as Parmeneides himself is concerned, the fact that the best evidence for this direct link between incubation and lawgiving comes from Crete is rather significant. In the whole Greek world there are two particular places that offer the closest of parallels for the *kouros* rituals once practised on Crete. One is Miletus.

The other is the town of Phocaea.

AND THOSE *KOUROS* TRADITIONS once known in Crete or other places—they never died out. After all, it would be strange if what has to do with things that never change wasn't essentially to stay the same.

You find them again in the East, surviving in traditions that grew up around the figure known in Persian as *javânmard*, in Arabic as *fatâ*. Both words mean 'young man', just like the Greek *kouros*.

Literally they were used, exactly the same as *kouros* in ancient Greek, for referring to someone under thirty years old. But in practice the words also had a far wider and much more technical meaning.

A *fatâ* or *javânmard* was the man of any age who's gone beyond time, who through the intensity of longing has made the initiatory journey outside of time and space and come to the heart of reality; who's found what never ages or dies.

Among Sufis and other mystics, especially in Persia, it was explained that there's never a time when these 'young men' don't exist somewhere on earth. The tradition they belong to is kept alive in a line of continuous succession that isn't tied to any particular country, or religion. And it's kept alive for one very simple reason: because the world we live in couldn't survive without them. They're the prophets, often ignored and almost always misunderstood, who keep existing because they have to.

It's only through them that the thread connecting humanity with reality stays intact. They have the responsibility of making the hero's journey into another world, to the source of light in the darkness, and bringing back the timeless knowledge that they find there. Without this knowledge or guidance, people would be totally deaf and blind. They'd be completely lost in their own confusion.

To a great extent this figure of the *javânmard* or *fatâ* has its origin in the ancient heroic traditions of the Iranians. But it had other origins as well. One of the most significant was the traditions about early Greek philosophy that were carried down from Alexandria into the Egyptian desert and sometimes kept alive for centuries by small groups of alchemists before being passed on to the East—into the Arab and Persian worlds.

Seen through the eyes of Arab alchemists, or Persian mystics, the earliest Greek philosophers weren't just thinkers or rationalists. They were links in an initiatory chain of succession. It was only later that their teachings were gradually swamped by intellectualism: that 'the traces of the paths of the ancient sages disappeared' and 'their directions were either wiped out, or corrupted and distorted'.

As for what those philosophers once wrote, it was expressed in riddles because they weren't interested in giving easy or theoretical answers. Their concern was to make you realize inside yourself what others might simply think or talk about. They had the power to transform people, to lead them through a process of death and rebirth to what lies beyond the human condition; to bring orphans back into the family they'd always belonged to.

And in addition to all this, they were understood as performing one particular role.

It was said that they'd been lawgivers—not just any kind of lawgiver but lawgivers who are prophets, who've received their laws from another world.

A Matter of Practicalities

THE IDEA OF PEOPLE RECEIVING LAWS THROUGH dreams or other states of awareness, of being given them in another world: this is as remote as possible from what we nowadays consider reality. In fact it's so remote that we can hardly believe such an idea could ever have been more than just that—an idea. And yet it was.

But even to go so far as to admit that once it was a reality in the West isn't enough. It's still to miss the point. That reality isn't anything at all like the one we're used to; and this is why at such a deep level we feel the need to deny its existence. For the fact is that we're up against something we simply don't understand.

TO US nothing could seem more absurdly impractical than the idea of creating new laws by lying in total silence and stillness. But from the point of view of people who once did this, it's our own ideas of practicality that are totally impractical.

We think that being practical means keeping busy getting on with our lives, rushing from one distraction to another, finding more and more substitutes for what we dimly sense but don't know how to face or discover. It's here that the problems come in—problems in understanding our past as well as ourselves.

The situation is exactly the same when it comes to making sense of Parmeneides' own teaching in his poem.

Some time ago a writer took the trouble to state in so many words what no other historian would dare to doubt, or would even bother to mention. He wrote that 'there is not the slightest indication' of Parmeneides' philosophy having any possible bearing on our lives and what we do with our lives, on the practicalities of our life-career and life-style: that his teaching is purely speculative and theoretical.

And yet Parmeneides himself offers a very different picture. There's nothing theoretical or impractical at all in how—even before starting his explanation of reality—he describes the imaginary road 'that human beings wander along, knowing nothing', going absolutely nowhere:

For helplessness in their chests is what steers their wandering minds
as they're carried along in a daze, deaf and blind at the same time,
indistinguishable, undistinguishing crowds.

On the contrary, what he's saying is so practical that it undermines every notion we have about what practicality really is. If you take it seriously, you can never live your life the same way again.

At first sight there's something rather alarming about how, over the centuries, scholars have developed the most sophisticated techniques for avoiding the simple implication of what Parmeneides says. Some have claimed—with total disregard for his own words—that he's not talking about people in general, that he's just criticizing one or two philosophers. Others see how absurd this explanation is, and accept that he's referring to human beings as a whole.

And there are even those who with measured reasonableness spell out the conclusion that the humans Parmeneides is referring to are clearly 'ordinary' mortals, 'who only see their daily surroundings but cannot see through them'.

But in all the time that's been spent studying Parmeneides' poem, analyzing it and arguing and writing about it, nobody has ever dared to ask one straightforward question. Could he possibly be referring to us?

In fact it's not so alarming that this very practical question hasn't ever been asked. It's not alarming at all, because it confirms in the most direct way possible just how accurate Parmeneides' description is.

Our wandering minds are so restless that they keep rushing this way and that, carrying us from theory to theory, from one sophisticated explanation to another. But they don't have the stillness that would ever allow the focus of our awareness to settle for more than the briefest moment on ourselves.

That's why, after more than two thousand years of arguing and theorizing and reasoning, still no one is able to agree for very long with anybody else about anything important. And it's why no amount of thinking will ever get us to the point of seeing the truth about ourselves— unless it brings us to the point of realizing that something else is needed.

ANY UNDERSTANDING of what Parmeneides' teaching originally meant or represented soon vanished in the West.

But even so, a general awareness that it once had contained something very real—and profoundly practical—continued to spread through the ancient world like ripples on water.

There's one peculiar statement in an ancient text that always meets with a mixture of embarrassment and silence. It's a statement that makes no sense at all if Parmeneides was only a theoretical philosopher.

The text talks quite simply about the supreme wisdom of trying, 'in word but also in action, to live a Pythagorean and Parmenidean way of life'. And it goes on to say that, for each of us, our whole life is a riddle waiting to be solved. The writer adds that really there's no greater danger or conceivable risk than failing to solve the riddle—in our lives and through them.

The mention of a Pythagorean as well as Parmenidean way of life might seem helpful in understanding what's involved. But even that has come to mean almost nothing. Nowadays it's usually assumed that Pythagoreans were little more than impractical dreamers, their minds fogged and obsessed with mysticism because all that interested them was the existence of some nebulous other world.

And yet the reality was very different. Even the words we've become most familiar with still have their own story to tell. The evidence indicates that the first Greeks who ever coined the word 'philosophy' in the technical sense of love of wisdom were Pythagoreans—which is hardly surprising, considering their fondness for coining new words or giving existing ones new meanings.

But for them philosophy hadn't become what it is for us. To them it was something that involved the whole of their being, that led to completeness and freedom. There were no half measures: wisdom demands everything you are.

We can still see examples of what that used to mean. The man who happens to have played the role of host when Plato travelled out to southern Italy to visit the Pythagoreans is sometimes pictured in modern literature as a quaint old eccentric, someone who loved spending his time inventing toys for children. And it's quite true that he was an inventor. As a matter of fact he was one of a number of Pythagoreans who used to be mechanical designers and engineers.

He also governed the city he lived in; and he was the commander of one of the most powerful armies in Italy. For the Pythagoreans fought if necessary to defend their lives and laws and traditions—against local tribes, also against the Athenian threat.

And they fought in ways we have no idea of any more. The early history of weaponry in the West developed through them. They invented types of artillery, based on principles of harmony and balance, that remained the standard form of weapon for almost two thousand years. To them even war was a great harmony— played by the artillery commander, heard in the catapult strings.

As far as they were concerned, harmony wasn't some celestial ideal. And it had nothing at all to do with sentimental ideas of sweetness and peace.

ONE OTHER REPORT about Parmeneides' teaching is worth mentioning, too. It has to do with Zeno—and Zeno's death.

There used to be many stories about how he died, in complete silence, under torture; but common to all the versions is the central theme of him being murdered by a local tyrant when he was caught leading an armed conspiracy. And one ancient writer makes a statement that's been translated as explaining how, when Zeno saw his life was over, he 'committed the work of Parmenides to the flames as being precious as pure gold'.

And yet the original Greek doesn't quite mean that. What it does say is that, through his suffering, 'he tested Parmenides' teaching in fire like gold that's pure and true'.

You might think this is all romantic invention—especially as the stories contain features typical of accounts about the heroism of Pythagorean women and men in the face of death. But as some scholars have realized, there are very particular details in the stories of Zeno's death that show they're basically no fantasy at all; and recent archaeological discoveries quite close to Sicily have made it even clearer that inside them there's a definite kernel of truth.

To be more precise: the details indicate that Zeno died smuggling arms out of Velia to help the people on a small, volcanic island just off the coast of Sicily defend themselves against the advancing power of Athens.

And of course, as we all know, Athens won the day.

FIVE

Invisible Lightning

PERHAPS YOU'VE NOTICED IT OUT OF THE corner of your eye—how even the most seemingly ordinary events can sometimes have such an immense significance they slip right through our awareness. And sometimes things can come to light, discoveries are made, that literally make no sense. The brain hardly registers them, or just refuses to register them at all.

The situation could be compared to thunder and lightning out in the countryside, so intense they can't be seen or heard: invisible lightning, silent thunder. Our minds simply won't acknowledge what's happened. And it's not only that everything seems to go on exactly as it did before; we're not even conscious of anything happening.

But there, where our awareness doesn't yet want to reach—that's where the future lies.

The archaeologists are still digging at Velia, measuring the ancient streets, mapping out the remains of old buildings down to the nearest fraction of an inch. Everything goes on as it did before.

And as to those inscriptions for Parmeneides and the Oulis healers, and for the Ouliadês who was a Iatromantis: they're little more than statistics now, inventory numbers that might as well never have existed. Really there's no need to go on pushing the evidence aside any more. It's already forgotten; past history. But just for safekeeping everything's been stored away in dark warehouses, well out of the public's sight and reach.

You might be tempted to describe the way that Parmeneides and the people close to him have been treated in the last two thousand years as a conspiracy, a conspiracy of silence. And in a very basic sense you'd be right.

But at the same time all these dramas of misrepresentation, of misuse and abuse, are nothing compared with what's been done to the central part of his teachings—or the writings of his successors. And the dramas fade away almost into insignificance compared with the extraordinary power of those teachings as they still survive: a power that's waiting to be understood again and used, not just talked about or pushed aside. This is what we'll need to explore next, and start rediscovering step by step.

So everything that's been mentioned so far—Parmeneides' opening account of his journey to another world, the traditions about him, the finds at Velia—may seem a story in itself or even a story within a story. But the story is far from finished, and this book that you've come to the end of is only the beginning: the first chapter.

REFERENCES

ABBREVIATIONS

APMM	P. Kingsley, *Ancient philosophy, mystery and magic* (revised ed., Oxford 1996)
Ascl.	E. J. and L. Edelstein, *Asclepius* (Baltimore 1945)
BCH	*Bulletin de Correspondance hellénique* (Paris)
Burkert	W. Burkert, 'Das Proömium des Parmenides und die Katabasis des Pythagoras', *Phronesis* 14 (1969) 1–30
Deubner	L. Deubner, *De incubatione* (Leipzig 1900)
Diels	H. Diels, *Parmenides, Lehrgedicht* (Berlin 1897)
DK	H. Diels and W. Kranz, *Die Fragmente der Vorsokratiker* (6th ed., Berlin 1951–2)
D.L.	Diogenes Laertius, *Lives of the philosophers*
EP	*Études sur Parménide*, ed. P. Aubenque (Paris 1987)
Fabbri–Trotta	M. Fabbri and A. Trotta, *Una scuola-collegio di età augustea* (Rome 1989) .
FS	*Filosofia e scienze in Magna Grecia. Atti del quinto convegno di studi sulla Magna Grecia* (Naples 1966)
Kingsley (1990)	'The Greek origin of the sixth-century dating of Zoroaster', *Bulletin of the School of Oriental and African Studies* 53 (1990) 245–65
Kingsley (1993)	'Poimandres. The etymology of the name and the origins of the Hermetica', *Journal of the Warburg & Courtauld Institutes* 56 (1993) 1–24
Kingsley (1994a)	'From Pythagoras to the *Turba philosophorum*', *Journal of the Warburg & Courtauld Institutes* 57 (1994) 1–13

235

Kingsley (1994b)   'Greeks, shamans and Magi', *Studia Iranica* 23
                     (1994) 187–98

Kingsley (1995)   'Meetings with Magi', *Journal of the Royal Asiatic
                     Society* 5 (1995) 173–209

LIMC   *Lexicon iconographicum mythologiae classicae* (Zurich
                     1981–97)

LS   W. Burkert, *Lore and science in ancient Pythagoreanism*
                     (Cambridge, MA 1972)

Mourelatos   A. P. D. Mourelatos, *The route of Parmenides* (New
                     Haven, Conn. 1970)

PGM   K. Preisendanz and A. Henrichs, *Papyri graecae magicae*
                     (Stuttgart 1973–4); *The Greek magical papyri in
                     translation*, ed. H. D. Betz (2nd ed., Chicago 1992)

PP   *La Parola del Passato* (Naples)

RE   G. Wissowa, W. Kroll *et al.*, *Paulys Realencyclopädie der
                     classischen Altertumswissenschaft* (Stuttgart and Munich
                     1894–1978)

Rohde   E. Rohde, *Psyche* (London 1925)

SEG   *Supplementum epigraphicum Graecum* (Leiden)

Phocaea

Phocaeans and the West: E. Langlotz, *Die kulturelle und künstlerische Hellenisierung der Küsten des Mittelmeers durch die Stadt Phokaia* (Cologne 1966); R. Carpenter, *Beyond the Pillars of Hercules* (London 1973) 45–67, 101–2, 143–98; J. Boardman, *The Greeks overseas* (3rd ed., London 1980) 214. And the East: Langlotz 11–13, 26–8.

Phocaea and trade: Aristotle, fragment 560 (Gigon); E. Lepore, *PP* 25 (1970) 19–54. Phocaea, Samos and the far west: Herodotus, *Histories* 1.163, 4.152; J.-P. Morel, *PP* 21 (1966) 390 n. 43, *BCH* 99 (1975) 892 n. 144 and in *Le Pont-Euxin vu par les Grecs*, ed. O. Lordkipanidzé and P. Lévêque (Paris 1990) 16. And Egypt: Herodotus 2.178, 4.152; Kingsley (1994a) 2–3; G. Schmidt, *Kyprische Bildwerke aus dem Heraion von Samos* (*Samos*, vii; Bonn 1968) 113–16, 119; U. Jantzen, *Ägyptische und orientalische Bronzen aus dem Heraion von Samos* (*Samos*, viii; Bonn 1972). Pythagoras' travels: Kingsley (1990), (1994a). His father: Kingsley (1994a) 2; Porphyry, *Life of Pythagoras* 1; Iamblichus, *The Pythagorean life* 2 (6.26–8.13 Deubner). His trousers: Kingsley (1994b) 192. Theodorus in Egypt: Schmidt 114, 139–40; Jantzen 91. Theodorus and Persia: H. Luschey, *Archaeologische Mitteilungen aus Iran*, new series 1 (1968) 88–9. Samos and Persia: Kingsley (1994b) 192. Telephanes: Boardman 103.

Travel in the Middle Ages: N. Ohler, *The medieval traveller* (Rochester, NY 1995). Greeks in Persia: R. T. Hallock, *Persepolis fortification tablets* (Chicago 1969) 349, 644, 722; C. Nylander, *Ionians at Pasargadae* (Uppsala 1970); M. Roaf, *Iran* 18 (1980) 70–2; Boardman 102–5; Kingsley (1994b), (1995). Pythagoras' 'discoveries': *APMM* 331. Egyptian models for Hera's temple: G. Shipley, *A history of Samos* (Oxford 1987) 57–8, 73. Dedications to Gula: Burkert in *The Greek Renaissance of the eighth century B.C.*, ed. R. Hägg (Stockholm 1983) 118. Copying of Babylonian imagery: Boardman 74, 77. Samians and Babylonia: C. Roebuck, *Ionian trade and colonization* (New York 1959) 6–8, 67–8; G. L. Huxley, *The early Ionians* (London 1966) 64; Boardman 62–77, 270 n. 121; Nylander 127; S. Dalley, *The legacy of Mesopotamia* (Oxford 1998) 98, 104, 107. 'Trade' and 'inquiry': Kingsley (1994a) 1–2. Non-Greek objects in Hera's temple: Jantzen; Morel, *BCH* 99 (1975) 892 n. 144; H. Kyrieleis, *Jahrbuch des Deutschen Archäologischen Instituts* 94 (1979) 32–48 and in *Greek sanctuaries*, ed. N. Marinatos and R. Hägg (London 1993) 145–9. Peacocks: J. Pollard, *Birds in Greek life and myth* (London 1977) 91–3.

Babylon under Persian rule: M. W. Stolper, *Entrepreneurs and empire* (Istanbul 1985); *Achaemenid history* iv, ed. H. Sancisi-Weerdenburg and A. Kuhrt (Leiden 1990) 184–7; Kingsley (1990). Babylonia, Persia, India: D. Pingree in *Studies in honor of Åke W. Sjöberg* (Philadelphia 1989) 439–45; Kingsley (1995) 198–208. Greeks in Babylonia: E. Weidner in *Mélanges syriens offerts à M. René Dussaud* ii (Paris 1939) 933; *Reallexikon der Assyriologie* iii (Berlin 1971) 645 and v (1980) 150; *Répertoire géographique des textes cunéiformes* viii (Wiesbaden 1985) 186–8. Later Greeks in Babylonia: G. K. Sarkisian, *Acta antiqua* 22 (1974) 495–503; *Hellenism in the East*, ed. A. Kuhrt and S. Sherwin-White (London 1987) 18–21, 50–1, 64–70. Indians and Carians in Babylonia: *Cambridge Ancient History* iv (2nd ed., Cambridge 1988) 133. The Carian in India: ibid., 201–5, 223, 479. Greeks, foreign languages and foreigners: Kingsley (1993), (1994a), (1994b).

Journey to the West

From Phocaea to Velia: Herodotus, *Histories* 1.162–7; M. Gigante, *PP* 21 (1966) 295–315; J.-P. Morel, *BCH* 99 (1975) 858 n. 22. Religion and the Persian expansion: Kingsley (1995) 191–5. Iron in the sea: Herodotus 1.165; C. A. Faraone, *Journal of Hellenic Studies* 113 (1993) 79–80. 'We promised to love …': *The erotic spirit*, ed. S. Hamill (Boston 1996) 49 (T'ang Dynasty). Ambiguity of oracles: W. B. Stanford, *Ambiguity in Greek literature* (Oxford 1939) 115–28.

Fairy Story

Confirmations of Herodotus: *PP* 21 (1966) 394 (Corsica) and *BCH* 99 (1975) 892 n. 144 (Samos); N. Cahill, *American Journal of Archaeology* 92 (1988) 500 and Ö. Özyiğit, *Kazı sonuçları toplantısı* 13/2 (1991) 104–5 (Phocaea); Fabbri–Trotta 71 and *APMM* 225 n., 392 (Velia). Truth and the Muses: Hesiod, *Theogony* 27–8. 'The wise': *APMM* 149–71 (as Pythagoreans, 162–3). Colonists and the Delphic oracle: P. Londey in *Greek colonists and native populations*, ed. J.-P. Descœudres (Oxford 1990) 117–27. Oracles as seeds: *APMM* 230–1, 299, 363 n. 12. Colonists, oracles and heroes: J. Bérard, *La colonisation grecque de l'Italie méridionale et de la Sicile* (2nd ed., Paris 1957); *Annali della Scuola Normale Superiore di Pisa, Classe di lettere e filosofia*, Series 3, 2/1 (1972) 35–104. Posidonia and Heracles: J. Jehasse, *Revue des études anciennes* 64 (1962) 252; J. G. Pedley, *Paestum* (London 1990) 66–7. Imitation of the hero: *APMM* 250–77, 297 n. 27. Love of wisdom, love of talking about wisdom: *APMM* 157–8.

What's Missing

'The central problem': K. von Fritz, *Gnomon* 14 (1938) 91–2. Greek philosophy and the East: Burkert, *Wiener Studien* 107/108 (1994/95) 179–86; Kingsley (1994a), (1994b), (1995) with n. 171, *Journal of the Royal Asiatic Society* 2 (1992) 345 and *Classical Review* 44 (1994) 294–6. Magicians: *APMM*.

Killing the Father

Dating of Parmenides: Plato, *Parmenides* 127b (*peri ... malista*); D.L. 9.23; E. Zeller, *A history of Greek philosophy* (London 1881) i 580–2; F. Jacoby, *Apollodors Chronik* (Berlin 1902) 231–6; W. Leszl in *Magna Grecia*, ed. G. Pugliese Carratelli (Milan 1988) 211 n. 115. Death at 60: *APMM* 1 n. Plato's *Parmenides* as fiction: J. Mansfeld, *Studies in the historiography of Greek philosophy* (Assen 1990) 64–7; C. H. Kahn, *Plato and the Socratic dialogue* (Cambridge 1996) 34. Belittling of Zeno: M. H. Miller Jr., *Plato's 'Parmenides'* (Princeton, NJ 1986) 28–34. Parmenides and Zeno as lovers: Plato, *Parmenides* 127b, 128a; K. J. Dover, *Greek homosexuality* (London 1978) 154; Miller 28. Teachers and disciples as lovers: Jacoby 233 n. 7; A.-P. Segonds in *Porphyre: Vie de Pythagore, Lettre à Marcella*, ed. É. des Places (Paris 1982) 182 n. 1, 187–8; *EP* ii 265 n. 62. Disregard for history in Plato's circle: Kingsley (1990) 263. Plato's disregard for it: R. Waterfield, *Plato: Republic* (Oxford 1993) 380, *Plato: Symposium* (1994) 77–8, 82, *Plato: Gorgias* (1994) 143; Kahn 34–5. Mythology into chronology: Kingsley (1995) 189–95. History writing as free enterprise: Kingsley (1990) 261–4. Precision and guessing: Burkert in *The ages of Homer*, ed. J. B. Carter and S. P. Morris (Austin, TX 1995) 146. 'He seemed to me ...': Plato, *Theaetetus* 183e–184a; J. Labarbe, *L'Homère de Platon* (Liège 1949) 329–30. Murder of 'father' Parmenides: Plato, *Sophist* 241d–242a; *EP* ii 3, 216. Platonic jokes: *APMM* 165–70. Patricide in ancient Greece: *Interpretations of Greek mythology*, ed. J. Bremmer (London/Sydney 1987) 49; *APMM* 101.

Getting Started

Parmenides and the feminine: P. Merlan, *Kleine philosophische Schriften* (Hildesheim 1976) 15–17. His descent to the underworld: J. S. Morrison, *Journal of Hellenic Studies* 75 (1955) 59–60; Burkert; M. E. Pellikaan-Engel, *Hesiod and Parmenides* (Amsterdam 1974); M. H. Miller Jr., *Apeiron* 13 (1979) 28–9; M. C. Nussbaum, *Harvard Studies in Classical Philology* 83

(1979) 69; D. Gallop, *Parmenides of Elea* (Toronto 1984) 6–7; M. M. Sassi, *PP* 43 (1988) 383–96 and in *Atti del ventottesimo convegno di studi sulla Magna Grecia* (Taranto 1989) 264; D. Furley, *Cosmic problems* (Cambridge 1989) 27–9; G. Cerri, *PP* 50 (1995) 458–67; *APMM* 54, 252 n. 6. Poetic suspense: Diels 22–3; G. E. Duckworth, *Foreshadowing and suspense in the epics of Homer, Apollonius, and Vergil* (Princeton, NJ 1933); A. H. Coxon, *The fragments of Parmenides* (Assen 1986) 159. Mansions of Night, gates of Night and Day, chasm of Tartarus: Hesiod, *Theogony* 736–66. Hinting and poetic tradition: *APMM* 42–5, 126–9. 'The mares that carry me ...': DK § 28 B1. 'Through the vast and dark unknown': S. Karsten, *Parmenidis Eleatae carminis reliquiae* (Amsterdam 1835) 54–5 (*kata pant' adaê: kata pant' atê, kata pantatê, kata panta tê* in manuscripts) with DK § 28 B8.59 (*nukt' adaê: nukt' ada ê, nuktada ê, nukta d' adaê* in manuscripts) and *EP* ii 209.

The Man in a Toga

The discoveries: M. Napoli, *FS* 140–2; M. Leiwo, *Arctos* 16 (1982) 46–8; Fabbri–Trotta 69–77; G. Pugliese Carratelli, *Tra Cadmo e Orfeo* (Bologna 1990) 269–71; *Velia: Studi e ricerche*, ed. G. Greco and F. Krinzinger (Modena 1994) 42–3. Oulis: P. Ebner, *Apollo* 2 (1962) 125–33; Pugliese Carratelli, *PP* 18 (1963) 385; Fabbri–Trotta 23. Apollo 'the healer': Ebner 132; M. Torelli in *Atti del ventisettesimo convegno di studi sulla Magna Grecia* (Taranto 1988) 62–5; Burkert, *The orientalizing revolution* (Cambridge, MA 1992) 78 and in *Apollo*, ed. J. Solomon (Tucson 1994) 55. 'Apollo. For he was a healer': *Suda*, under 'Oulios'; *RE* Supplementband xiv (1974) 930–1. Apollo at Phocaea: F. Bilabel, *Die ionische Kolonisation* (Leipzig 1920) 243–4; F. Graf, *Nordionische Kulte* (Rome 1985) 410. Religious traditions from Phocaea to Velia: Herodotus, *Histories* 1.164, 166; Fabbri–Trotta 71; *APMM* 225 n. 28, 392. History and distribution of the words Oulis, Oulios: O. Masson, *Journal des Savants* (1988) 173–81; G. Manganaro, *Chiron* 22 (1992) 385–94 with 386 n. 5.

Dying Before You Die

'Hard fate': Burkert 14, 25; Mourelatos 15; M. E. Pellikaan-Engel, *Hesiod and Parmenides* (Amsterdam 1974) 60–1; A. H. Coxon, *The fragments of Parmenides* (Assen 1986) 10, 16, 167; M. M. Sassi, *PP* 43 (1988) 389; *APMM* 54–5 n. 15, 252 n. 6. Heracles' welcome and initiation: Diodorus Siculus 4.26.1; Burkert 5; R. J. Clark, *Catabasis* (Amsterdam 1979) 90–1, 208. 'The man who knows': Burkert 5.

Justice: Sophocles, *Antigone* 451; E. Maass, *Orpheus* (Munich 1895) 232, 269–71; O. Gilbert, *Archiv für Geschichte der Philosophie* 20 (1907) 35–6; M. P. Nilsson, *The Dionysiac mysteries of the Hellenistic and Roman age* (Lund 1957) 121–5; *LIMC* iii/1 (1986) 388–91; Sassi 388–9; *SEG* 40 (1990) § 907; G. Cerri, *PP* 50 (1995) 462–3. Orphic traditions at Velia: DK i 2.2; Burkert 17; Sassi 383–96; B. Otto in *Akten des XIII. Internationalen Kongresses für Klassische Archäologie* (Mainz am Rhein 1990) 400; *SEG* 40 (1990) § 904. Orphic cave of Night: O. Kern, *Archiv für Geschichte der Philosophie* 3 (1890) 173–4; M. L. West, *The Orphic poems* (Oxford 1983) 109, 213–14. 'Kindly': G. Zuntz, *Persephone* (Oxford 1971) 302–5 (*prophrôn*), 317 n. 2; A. M. Kropp, *Ausgewählte koptische Zaubertexte* ii (Brussels 1931) 21. Right hand in the underworld: O. Weinreich, *Antike Heilungswunder* (Giessen 1909) 41–5; Kropp 17–18; Zuntz 367; West, *Zeitschrift für Papyrologie und Epigraphik* 18 (1975) 229–30; C. Brăiloiu, *Problems of ethnomusicology* (Cambridge 1984) 295; W. M. Brashear, *Magica varia* (Brussels 1991) 43. Orphic gold texts: *APMM* 250–316. Initiation, adoption, children of the gods: Rohde 601–3.

No cities: Coxon, *Classical Quarterly* 18 (1968) 69; J. Mansfeld, *Die Offenbarung des Parmenides und die menschliche Welt* (Assen 1964) 224–5; Burkert 6 n. 14. Darkness and ignorance: C. H. Kahn, *Gnomon* 42 (1970) 116; J. Owens, *The Monist* 62/1 (1979) 19.

Underworld as place of paradox: *APMM* 77. Sun and underworld: A. Laumonier, *Les cultes indigènes en Carie* (Paris 1958) 580; Burkert 9, 21; Otto 400 (Velia); Cerri 444–5; *APMM* 49–68. Pythagoreans, volcanic regions, Platonists: *APMM* 50–213. Christians and Jewish mystics: N. Terzaghi, *Synesii Cyrenensis hymni* (Rome 1949) 170; G. G. Stroumsa in *Death, ecstasy and other worldly journeys*, ed. J. J. Collins and M. Fishbane (New York 1995) 139–54. Alchemists: *APMM* 49–68. 'Reaching up into the heavens': Pellikaan-Engel 57; *APMM* 18 n. 14, 252 n. 6. Atlas: Pellikaan-Engel 31–2, 55. Descent, ascent and cosmic axis: *APMM* 252 n. 6.

Age of *kouros*: H. Jeanmaire, *Couroi et Courètes* (Lille 1939) 32–7. His journey to the beyond: ibid., 330–1. Heracles as *kouros*: Burkert 14 n. Nameless *kouros*, nameless goddess: D. Sabbatucci, *Saggio sul misticismo greco* (Rome 1965) 208–9. *Kouros* and prophecy, oracles, dreams: Aristophanes, *Birds* 977 with C. A. Faraone, *Classical Quarterly* 42 (1992) 320–7; *PGM* VII.679–80; T. Hopfner in *Recueil d'études, dédiées à la mémoire de N. P. Kondakov* (Prague 1926) 65–6; W. J. Verdenius, *Mnemosyne* 13 (1947) 285. 'Second destiny': Rohde 602 (*deuteropotmos*). Initiation and rebirth in Italy: T. H. Price, *Kourotrophos* (Leiden 1978) 39 (Heracles); B. M. Fridh-Haneson in *Gifts to the gods*, ed. T. Linders and G. Nordquist (Uppsala 1987) 67–75; *APMM* 250–77.

Divine *kouros* and *kourai*, Apollo: A. Brelich, *Paides e parthenoi* i (Rome 1969) 435–6; West, *Hesiod, Theogony* (Oxford 1966) 263–4 and *Hesiod, Works and Days* (1978) 372. Humans as children of the sun: DK i 218.2–3; A. Delatte, *La Vie de Pythagore de Diogène Laërce* (Brussels 1922) 210; P. Boyancé in *Mélanges Carcopino* (Paris 1966) 153 n.

Masters of Dreams

Latin Phôlarchos inscriptions: Fabbri–Trotta 70, 77. The Greek dictionaries: *PP* 25 (1970) 214, 245; M. Leiwo, *Arctos* 16 (1982) 50; Burkert 22 n. 51. Meanings of *phôleos, phôleia, phôleuein*: S. Musitelli, *PP* 35 (1980) 241–55. Modern science, ancient magic: *APMM* 217–32, 294–6. 'On the road...': Strabo, *Geography* 14.1.44; A. Brelich, *Gli eroi greci* (Rome 1958) 215–16; H. Brewster, *Classical Anatolia* (London 1993) 49–50. Hierapolis, Acharaca and Apollo: J. H. Croon, *Herdsman of the dead* (Utrecht 1952) 75–9. Apollo and incubation: Deubner 32–8, 55–6 n.; C. Dugas, *BCH* 34 (1910) 235–40; W. Deonna, *Revue de l'histoire des religions* 83 (1921) 166–8; *Ascl.* ii 99, 191 n. 1; S. Eitrem, *Orakel und Mysterien am Ausgang der Antike* (Zurich 1947) 51–2; F. Graf, *Nordionische Kulte* (Rome 1985) 250–5. At Hierapolis: Damascius, *Life of Isidorus* 131 (... *enkatheudêsas* ...) with Deubner 6–7 (*enkatheudein*). In magic: Eitrem 51–2. Miletus and Phocaea: *RE* i/1 (1894) 2362 § 5 and i/2 (1896) 113 (Apollonia); *Der Neue Pauly* i (1996) 592 (Amisus); F. Bilabel, *Die ionische Kolonisation* (Leipzig 1920) 14, 29. Priests of Apollo the healer at Istria: S. Lambrino, *Archaiologikê Ephêmeris* (1937) 352–62. Apollo Phôleutêrios: D. M. Pippidi in *Stêlê: tomos eis mnêmên Nikolaou Kontoleontos* (Athens 1980) 40–3 ('I confess...'); *SEG* 30 (1980) §§ 798, 1225; G. Sacco, *Rivista di filologia e di istruzione classica* 109 (1981) 36–40.

Apollo

Rationalizing of Apollo: K. Latte, *Harvard Theological Review* 33 (1940) 9–10; E. R. Dodds, *The Greeks and the irrational* (Berkeley 1956) 68–9. Of Asclepius: G. Vlastos, *Review of Religion* 13 (1948) 269–90. Incantatory language, trance and riddles: Burkert in *Apollo*, ed. J. Solomon (Tucson 1994) 49–60. Apollo at Rome: Deubner 32 n. 1. His priestess: Dodds 69–70. Apollo, caves, darkness, underworld and death: ibid., 91–2 n. 66; C. Schefer, *Platon und Apollon* (Sankt Augustin 1996) 10–17, 27–8, 162–74. The temples above a cave: J. H. Croon, *Herdsman of the dead* (Utrecht 1952) 76 (Hierapolis); *Archaeological Reports* (1959–60) 42–3, *LS* 145 n., 155, L. Robert, *Opera minora selecta* vi (Amsterdam 1989) 28–9 (Clarus).

Apollo and the sun: *Museum Helveticum* 7 (1950) 185–99 and 25 (1968) 182; P. Boyancé in *Mélanges Carcopino* (Paris 1966) 149–70; Burkert 21 and *Grazer Beiträge* 4 (1975) 73–4; *Der Kleine Pauly* i (1975) 446–7; F. Ahl, *American Journal of Philology* 103 (1982) 373–411; D. Metzler in *Antidoron: Festschrift für Jürgen Thimme* (Karlsruhe 1983) 75; *LIMC* ii/1 (1984) 244–6; Schefer 196–7.'The silent names ...': Euripides, fragment 775 (Nauck); Boyancé 151–2. Orpheus, Apollo, the sun: M. L. West, *The Orphic poems* (Oxford 1983) 12–13 and *Studies in Aeschylus* (Stuttgart 1990) 32–47; G. Colli, *La sagesse grecque* i (Combas 1990) 198–9. Orpheus, Apollo, Night: Plutarch, *Moral essays* 566b–c; *APMM* 133–8, 282–7.

Apollo making love to Persephone: West, *Orphic poems* 95, 98, 100. Healing and death: *Ascl.* i 106, ii 128–9, 215. Persephone's healing touch: O. Weinreich, *Antike Heilungswunder* (Giessen 1909) 11, 38. Hero-figures, Apollo and Persephone: *LS* 149–50 with n. 157 (Abaris); I. M. Linforth, *The arts of Orpheus* (Berkeley 1941) 4–5, 22–3, 28, 61–4, 192, 262–3 (Orpheus).

Goddess

Persephone's home: Hesiod, *Theogony* 736–74. Her right hand: *LIMC* viii/1 (1997) 972 §§ 272, 274. Anonymity of underworld divinities: Rohde 185; M. L. West, *Hesiod, Theogony* (Oxford 1966) 369–70; Burkert 13–14; M. Guarducci, *Atti della Accademia Nazionale dei Lincei, Rendiconti* 33 (1978) 274–6; *SEG* 30 (1980) § 326; A. M. Ardovino, *Archeologia classica* 32 (1980) 56; A. D. H. Bivar in *Studies in Mithraism*, ed. J. R. Hinnells (Rome 1994) 63. Anonymity of Persephone (outside Italy): Sophocles, *Oedipus Coloneus* 683, 1548; L. R. Farnell, *Cults of the Greek states* iii (Oxford 1907) 132–41; G. E. Mylonas, *Eleusis and the Eleusinian mysteries* (Princeton, NJ 1961) 198, 238; C. Kerényi, *Eleusis* (New York 1967) 26–9, 152–5; L. Polacco, *Numismatica e antichità classiche* 15 (1986) 28; K. Clinton, *Opuscula Atheniensia* 16 (1986) 44 and in *Greek sanctuaries*, ed. N. Marinatos and R. Hägg (London 1993) 113, 120, 124; *SEG* 40 (1990) § 1159; C. A. Faraone, *Talismans and Trojan horses* (New York 1992) 62 (oracle of Apollo); *APMM* 354. In Italy: *Corpus inscriptionum Graecarum* xiv (Berlin 1890) §§ 630, 644, 665; G. Giannelli, *Culti e miti della Magna Grecia* (Florence 1924) 127–8, 187–97; P. Zancani Montuoro, *Atti Acc. Naz. Linc., Rend.* 14 (1959) 225–8; Burkert 14 n. 31 and *LS* 113 n. 21; G. Zuntz, *Persephone* (Oxford 1971) 317 n. 1; M. L. Lazzarini, *Le formule delle dediche votive nella Grecia arcaica* (Rome 1976) 76, 205–6.

Velian dedication to Persephone: G. Antonini, *La Lucania* i (Naples 1795) 302–5; J. C. Orelli, *Inscriptionum Latinarum selectarum collectio* i (Zurich 1828) § 2512; *Corpus inscriptionum Latinarum* x (Berlin 1883) § 98*. The rock inscription: F. Ribezzo, *Rivista indo-greco-italica* 21 (1937) 210; P. Ebner, *Rivista Italiana di Numismatica* 51 (1949) 9–10; *PP* 21 (1966) 332, 337–8. Between Velia and Posidonia: *Corp. inscr. Lat.* x § 467. Persephone at Posidonia: Giannelli 127–8; J. G. Pedley, *Paestum* (London 1990) 20, 88–9, 99–100. Rome: G. Wissowa, *Religion und Kultus der Römer* (2nd ed., Munich 1912) 298; Burkert 22; J.-P. Morel, *BCH* 99 (1975) 864, 893. Velian worship of Persephone and Demeter from Phocaea: Ebner 10; F. Graf, *Nordionische Kulte* (Rome 1985) 418.

Iatromantis

The man from Crete: DK i 27–37; H. Demoulin, *Épiménide de Crète* (Brussels 1901); G. Colli, *La sagesse grecque* ii (Combas 1991) 44–75; *APMM* 284 n., 287 n. (Epimenides). Pythagoras and Anatolian traditions: Burkert 23–6; *LS* 155 n. 197 (Samos); *APMM* 225, 293–4, 331. Pythagoras, Pythagoreans, incubation: Hippolytus, *Refutation of all heresies* 1.2.18; *LS* 155–61; I. P. Culianu, *Studi storico religiosi* 4 (1980) 291, 294–5; *APMM* 282–8. Incubation and death: J. D. P. Bolton, *Aristeas of Proconnesus* (Oxford 1962) 153–6; *LS* 151–61; J. Hani, *Revue des études grecques* 88 (1975) 108–12; Culianu 295 and *Psychanodia* i (Leiden 1983) 44. Parmenides, incubation and experts at incubation: Diels 13–22; Demoulin 99; J. S. Morrison, *Journal of Hellenic Studies* 75 (1955) 59–60; *Gnomon* 35 (1963) 239–40; Burkert; *LS* 283–4; Culianu, *Studi storico religiosi* 4 (1980) 295, 300; A. Francotte in *Mélanges Ph. Marçais* (Paris 1985) 30–7.

Ecstasy

The inscription: *PP* 25 (1970) 247, 262. Ouliadês: L. Zgusta, *Kleinasiatische Personennamen* (Prague 1964) 398; P. Merlan, *Kleine philosophische Schriften* (Hildesheim 1976) 10; O. Masson, *Journal des Savants* (1988) 173–81. Iatromantis: Aeschylus, *Suppliant women* 260–70 ('son of Apollo'), *Eumenides* 61–3 (Apollo); Aristophanes, *Plutus* 8–11; Rohde 132–3; J. Vürtheim, *Aischylos' Schutzflehende* (Amsterdam 1928) 60–6; W. Kranz, *Empedokles* (Zurich 1949) 27; *Der Kleine Pauly* i (1975) 645; I. P. Culianu, *Studi storico religiosi* 4 (1980) 287–303; *APMM* 220 n.; *Der Neue Pauly* i (1996) 865–6.

Incantations: Plato, *Charmides* 155e–158c, *Republic* 364b–e; P. Laín Entralgo, *The therapy of the word in classical antiquity* (New Haven 1970);

A. Francotte in *Mélanges Ph. Marçais* (Paris 1985) 35–6; *APMM* 222, 247–8, 342. Breath control: M. Detienne, *La notion de daïmôn dans le Pythagorisme ancien* (Paris 1963) 76–85; J. P. Vernant, *Mythe et pensée chez les Grecs* (Paris 1965) 65–7, 85; L. Gernet, *Anthropologie de la Grèce antique* (Paris 1976) 424–5; Francotte 26–31.

Neither sleep nor waking: Plutarch, *Moral essays* 590b; Iamblichus, *On the mysteries* 3.2; K. H. E. de Jong, *De Apuleio Isiacorum mysteriorum teste* (Leiden 1900) 99–106; Deubner 4–5; R. Reitzenstein, *Poimandres* (Leipzig 1904) 12 n. 1, 361; *Ascl.* i 210–11, 255–6, ii 150; G. Vlastos, *Review of Religion* 13 (1948) 284–5; J. Leipoldt in *Aus Antike und Orient*, ed. S. Morenz (Leipzig 1950) 57; R. J. Clark, *Transactions of the American Philological Association* 99 (1968) 64, 73; J. Hani, *Revue des études grecques* 88 (1975) 110; Kingsley (1993) 15–16.

Apollo, space and time: Vürtheim 222; U. von Wilamowitz-Moellendorff, *Kleine Schriften* i (Berlin 1935) 497–8; Kingsley (1994b) 191 n. 15. Apollo and ecstasy, trance, catalepsy: K. Latte, *Harvard Theological Review* 33 (1940) 9–18; E. R. Dodds, *The Greeks and the irrational* (Berkeley 1956) 69–71; Clark 74; Culianu, *Psychanodia* i (Leiden 1983) 37. 'Taken by Apollo': Herodotus, *Histories* 4.13; Burkert, *Gnomon* 35 (1963) 239. 'Skywalker': *LS* 150 n., 162 n. (*aithrobatês*); M. Eliade, *Shamanism: archaic techniques of ecstasy* (Princeton, NJ 1964) 410; K. Dowman, *Sky dancer* (Ithaca, NY 1996) 224. Crete and Mesopotamia: Burkert, *The orientalizing revolution* (Cambridge, MA 1992) 60–3 (Epimenides); S. Dalley, *The legacy of Mesopotamia* (Oxford 1998) 86–8, 104. Greek shamanism and the East: K. Meuli, *Hermes* 70 (1935) 121–76; E. D. Phillips, *Artibus Asiae* 18 (1955) 161–77; *LS* 162–3; G. M. Bongard-Levin and E. A. Grantovskij, *De la Scythie à l'Inde* (Paris 1981); D. Metzler in *Antidoron: Festschrift für Jürgen Thimme* (Karlsruhe 1983) 75–82; J. Bremmer, *The early Greek concept of the soul* (Princeton, NJ 1983) 39–40; F. Graf, *Nordionische Kulte* (Rome 1985) 390, 392; Francotte 33 n. 2; C. Ginzburg, *Ecstasies* (London 1990) 207–95; P. Gignoux, *Les inscriptions de Kirdîr et sa vision de l'au-delà* (Rome 1990); Kingsley (1994b); *APMM* 224–7.

Turîya: Eliade, *Yoga: immortality and freedom* (New York 1958) 57 n., 99, 124. Parmenides and shamanism: Diels 14–15; Meuli 171–2; Burkert, *Gnomon* 35 (1963) 239–40 and *LS* 283–4; W. K. C. Guthrie, *A history of Greek philosophy* ii (Cambridge 1965) 11–12; Mourelatos 42–4; M. L. West, *Early Greek philosophy and the Orient* (Oxford 1971) 225–6; Metzler 78; Francotte 41–7; R. Böhme, *Die verkannte Muse* (Bern 1986) 113–17; M. Duichin, *Abstracta* 3/28 (1988) 28; Kingsley (1994b) 190 n. Apollo and shamanism: Phillips 176–7; Eliade, *Shamanism* 388; Hani 116–18; J. F. Kindstrand, *Anacharsis* (Uppsala 1981) 18–20; Metzler 75; Kingsley (1994b) 191.

The Sound of Piping

Aristotle on philosophical poetry: *APMM* 43–4, 53. The Platonists: DK i 220.30–43; Mourelatos 36 n. 77. 'Hard to excuse …': J. Barnes, *The Presocratic philosophers* (2nd ed., London 1982) 155. Modern praise for Parmenides' poetry: J. Beaufret, *Le poème de Parménide* (Paris 1955) 8; Mourelatos 224–5; A. Francotte in *Mélanges Ph. Marçais* (Paris 1985) 39. His use of sound: H. Pfeiffer, *Die Stellung des parmenideischen Lehrgedichtes in der epischen Tradition* (Bonn 1975) 187. Of metre and rhythm: Mourelatos 2, 264–8. Humour, word play, ambiguity: O. Kern, *Archiv für Geschichte der Philosophie* 3 (1890) 174; Mourelatos 156, 222–63. His oracular and initiatory language: C. H. Kahn, *Anaximander and the origins of Greek cosmology* (New York 1960) 227; M. Timpanaro Cardini, *Studi classici e orientali* 16 (1967) 171; Burkert 4–5; *APMM* 354. The language of initiation: *APMM* 360–3; *Parabola* 22/1 (1997) 21–2.

Starting where they started: *APMM* 6–7, 385. 'Naive' … 'expressive failure': Diels 23–4; Mourelatos 35. Poetic use of repetition: E. R. Dodds, *The Greeks and the irrational* (Berkeley 1956) 123 n. 20. Repetition and incantation: S. Eitrem, *Papyri Osloenses* i (Oslo 1925) 58–9; Dodds, *The ancient concept of progress* (Oxford 1973) 199–200; N. J. Richardson, *The Homeric Hymn to Demeter* (Oxford 1974) 61, 159, 229; W. M. Brashear, *Magica varia* (Brussels 1991) 42; C. A. Faraone, *Classical Journal* 89 (1993) 4–5.

Philosophy and words of power: *APMM* 222, 230–2, 247–8, 299, 361–3.

'He doesn't need …': P. Boyancé, *Le culte des Muses chez les philosophes grecs* (Paris 1936) 76.

'Song' and 'road': K. Meuli, *Hermes* 70 (1935) 172–3; W. K. C. Guthrie, *A history of Greek philosophy* ii (Cambridge 1965) 12–13. Shamanic background to Orphic tradition: Kingsley (1994b) 189–90; *APMM* 226. Shamanism, magic and Greek epic: Meuli 164–76; E. D. Phillips, *Artibus Asiae* 18 (1955) 176 n.; M. L. West, *Hesiod, Theogony* (Oxford 1966) 2–16. Repetition in shamanism: H. Munn in *Hallucinogens and shamanism*, ed. M. J. Harner (New York 1973) 86–122; *Shamanism*, ed. S. Nicholson (Wheaton, IL 1987) 3, 13, 91, 117–20.

'Reduction of appearances': Kahn, *Gnomon* 42 (1970) 118. The roots of existence: West 361–4.

Pythagorean silence: *LS* 178–9. Incubation, spinning, piping or whistling: Plutarch, *Moral essays* 590b–d; Iamblichus, *On the mysteries* 3.2; Deubner 10 (*rhoizos*). Parmenides' journey and *kundalinî*: *Symbolon* 7 (1971) 76 = O. M. Hinze, *Tantra vidyâ* (Delhi 1979) 107.

Recipe for immortality: *PGM* IV.475–829; A.-J. Festugière, *La révélation d'Hermès Trismégiste* i (2nd ed., Paris 1950) 303–8; G. Fowden, *The Egyptian Hermes* (Cambridge 1986) 82–4; *APMM* 221, 313, 374–5. Making the sound of a *syrinx*: *PGM* IV.561, 578; A. Dieterich, *Abraxas* (Leipzig 1891) 23 and *Eine Mithrasliturgie* (3rd ed., Leipzig 1923) 42. And breath control: *PGM* XIII.933–46. The sound of silence: Dieterich, *Mithraslit.* 42–3. 'I too am a star ...': *PGM* IV.574–5. The sound of creation: H. Lewy, *Chaldaean Oracles and theurgy* (2nd ed., Paris 1978) 18 n. 46, 85 n. 69, 110 n., 404 n. 12, 406 n. 22 (*rhoizos*). Sound of the stars and planets: Lewy 19 n., 193 n. 63, 255 n. 99, 256 n. 102, 412 n. 43; É. des Places, *Jamblique, Les mystères d'Égypte* (Paris 1966) 18, 109. Sound of the wind: *Orphic hymns* 34.25; *Orphicorum fragmenta*, fragment 297b (Kern); Macrobius, *Saturnalia* 1.21.9. Harmony of the spheres: Plutarch 590c–d; Iamblichus, *On the mysteries* 3.9 and *The Pythagorean life* 65; *LS* 357. 'There's no tearing one's heart away ...': Lewy 18 n. 46; ibid., 696 = Dodds, *Harvard Theological Review* 54 (1961) 266; H. Erbse, *Theosophorum Graecorum fragmenta* (2nd ed., Stuttgart/Leipzig 1995) 8 (Clarus).

Rebirth through the sun: *PGM* IV.639–49. 'Sun-runner': Dieterich, *Mithraslit.* 151; M. J. Vermaseren, *Mithras, the secret god* (London 1963) 151–2; *Studies in Mithraism*, ed. J. R. Hinnells (Rome 1994) 41, 110–13. Pipe hanging from the sun: *PGM* IV.544–55; C. G. Jung, *Symbols of transformation* (London 1956) 100–2 (*aulos*). Sun and pipes: Macrobius, *Saturnalia* 1.21.9; *Orphic hymns* 8.11(*syriktês*); Dieterich, *Abraxas* 24. Magical papyri, Italy and Sicily: *APMM* 217–391. Magical papyri, Apollo and Delphi: Dieterich, *Abraxas* 111–16.

Apollo and snakes: Aelian, *Nature of animals* 11.2; D.L. 5.91; Dieterich, *Abraxas* 114; *Museum Helveticum* 7 (1950) 192; *Der Kleine Pauly* iv (1975) 1280; K. Kerényi, *Apollon und Niobe* (Munich 1980) 377–83 = *Apollo* (Dallas, TX 1983) 38–44; *LIMC* ii/1 (1984) 230–1. Apollo as a snake: Deubner 32–3 n.; W. Deonna, *Revue de l'histoire des religions* 83 (1921) 167–8; Dieterich, *Abraxas* 114 n. 5; J. Fontenrose, *Python* (Berkeley 1959) 469–70, 492. Asclepius: Deubner 32 n.; *Ascl.* i 215/218, 258–9 (... *ti phrikôdes* ...).

Syrinx and *syrigmos* at Delphi: Dieterich, *Abraxas* 116; Fontenrose 453–8; West, *Ancient Greek music* (Oxford 1992) 102, 212–15. And *kouros*: H. Jeanmaire, *Couroi et Courètes* (Lille 1939) 407; A. Brelich, *Paides e parthenoi* i (Rome 1969) 387–91, 406–7, 432–6, 447–9.

Founding Hero

The Parmenides inscription: P. Ebner, *Rassegna Storica Salernitana* 23 (1962) 6, *Apollo* 2 (1962) 128–9 and *Illustrated London News*, 31 August 1963, 306; M. Napoli, *FS* 140–1. The Asclepius statue: V. Catalano, *Annali del Pontificio Istituto Superiore di Scienze e Lettere "Santa Chiara"* 15–16 (1965–66) 291–2; A. de Franciscis, *PP* 25 (1970) 268, 278, 283–4. Parmen(e)ides: M. Untersteiner, *Parmenide* (Florence 1958) 3–4; P. Merlan, *Kleine philosophische Schriften* (Hildesheim 1976) 9. Pyres: O. Masson, *Journal des Savants* (1988) 180.

Physikos: Aristotle, *On sense perception* 436a17–b1 and *On breathing* 480b22–30; Macrobius, *Saturnalia* 7.15.14–15; K. H. E. de Jong, *De Apuleio Isiacorum mysteriorum teste* (Leiden 1900) 56 n.; J. Röhr, *Der okkulte Kraftbegriff im Altertum* (Leipzig 1923) 77–85; M. Wellmann, *Die Physika des Bolos Demokritos und der Magier Anaxilaos aus Larissa* i (Berlin 1928); Catalano 298–9; *FS* 119–24; Ebner, *Giornale di metafisica* 21 (1966) 105; V. Nutton, *PP* 25 (1970) 223 and *Medical History* 15 (1971) 6–7; *RE* Supplementband xiv (1974) 929; M. Gigante, *PP* 43 (1988) 224; G. Pugliese Carratelli, *Tra Cadmo e Orfeo* (Bologna 1990) 279; *APMM* 229. Italian philosophy, practicality and healing: *APMM* 217–32, 317–47. Hippocratic writers: *On ancient medicine* 20; A.-J. Festugière, *Hippocrate: L'Ancienne Médecine* (Paris 1948) 60 n. 70; Pugliese Carratelli 279; C. A. Huffman, *Philolaus of Croton* (Cambridge 1993) 126; *APMM* 229–30. 'Not to teach but to heal': Aristotle, fragment 174 (Gigon); *APMM* 342.

Parmeneides' poem and medicine: Ebner, *Rassegna Storica Salernitana* 22 (1961) 197 and 23 (1962) 6 n.; Merlan 8–17; H. Jucker, *Museum Helveticum* 25 (1968) 183 n.; J. Benedum and M. Michler, *Clio medica* 6 (1971) 303–4; G. Rocca-Serra, *Histoire des sciences médicales* 19 (1985) 171–2; Fabbri–Trotta 75–6. Quoted by medical experts: Rocca-Serra 172. Head of a medical school: S. Musitelli, *Da Parmenide a Galeno* (Rome 1985).

Parmeneides as *hêrôs ktistês*: Jucker 183; Benedum–Michler 303; *RE* Supplementband xiv (1974) 933; Fabbri–Trotta 20, 72–3; F. Krinzinger, *Römische Historische Mitteilungen* 34/35 (1992/1993) 41. Priests of Apollo as heroes: A. Dieterich, *Kleine Schriften* (Leipzig 1911) 193–5; L. R. Farnell, *Greek hero cults and ideas of immortality* (Oxford 1921) 53–5; A. Laumonier, *Les cultes indigènes en Carie* (Paris 1958) 555; J. D. P. Bolton, *Aristeas of Proconnesus* (Oxford 1962) 129. Iatromantis figures as heroes: Bolton 120, 123; F. Graf, *Nordionische Kulte* (Rome 1985) 390–5.

The Line

Parmeneides adopts Zeno: D.L. 9.25 = Apollodorus, fragment 30 (Jacoby);
F. Jacoby, *Apollodors Chronik* (Berlin 1902) 231 n. 1; *LS* 180.
Adoption in Anatolia: A. Wentzel, *Hermes* 65 (1930) 167–76; A.
Laumonier, *Les cultes indigènes en Carie* (Paris 1958) 130–1, 227 n. 9, 282
n. 1; M. S. Smith, *Classical Quarterly* 17 (1967) 302–10. Anatolian priests
and healers, adoption and fosterage: A. Cameron in *Anatolian studies
presented to William Hepburn Buckler* (Manchester 1939) 32–4; R.
Merkelbach, *Roman und Mysterium in der Antike* (Munich 1962) 164–5.
Adoption and the Hippocratic school: C. J. de Vogel, *Pythagoras and
early Pythagoreanism* (Assen 1966) 239–41; *LS* 179; G. Rocca-Serra,
Histoire des sciences médicales 19 (1985) 172–3; Fabbri–Trotta 75; V.
Nutton and H. von Staden in *Médecine et morale dans l'antiquité* (*Entretiens
sur l'antiquité classique*, xliii; Vandœuvres/Geneva 1997) 196. Hippocrates,
Asclepius, Apollo: S. Sherwin-White, *Ancient Cos* (Göttingen 1978) 256–
89, 301–3, 338–60; J. Jouanna, *Journal des Savants* (1989) 17–22; G.
Pugliese Carratelli, *Tra Cadmo e Orfeo* (Bologna 1990) 276–7; von Staden
180, 185–91. Asklepiadês and Ouliadês: O. Masson, *Journal des Savants*
(1988) 180; *SEG* 39 (1989) § 1078.
Parmeneides and Zeno as Pythagoreans: *PP* 21 (1966) 329; *LS* 280
n. Pythagorean creativity and originality: *APMM* 92–3, 160, 182, 191–4,
199, 319, 328–34. Fluidity of Pythagorean tradition: Kingsley (1990)
261 and n. 99; *APMM* 328–34. Adoption in Pythagoreanism: L. Edelstein,
Ancient medicine (Baltimore 1967) 43–7, 57; de Vogel 240–1; *LS* 179–80,
294. Adoption and rebirth in the mysteries: A. Dieterich, *Eine Mithrasliturgie*
(3rd ed., Leipzig 1923) 134–55; Rohde 601–3; Merkelbach 165, 238; *LS*
179–80, 294; *APMM* 221. 'True fathers': Merkelbach 238 n. 4. Pythagorean
anonymity: *APMM* 163. Pythagoras and Apollo: *LS* 91, 141–6, 178.
'Father' Parmenides: Plato, *Sophist* 241d–242a; de Vogel 241; *LS*
180 n.; Rocca-Serra 173 and *EP* ii 266 n. 65. 'Father' in Pythagoreanism:
Edelstein 43–5; de Vogel 240; *LS* 179, 294. In mysteries: Dieterich 52,
134–43, 146–56; Rohde 602; R. Reitzenstein, *Die hellenistischen
Mysterienreligionen* (3rd ed., Leipzig 1927) 20, 40–1; Merkelbach 165,
238; Burkert, *Ancient mystery cults* (Cambridge, MA 1987) 42, 50, 99 and
LS 179–80; *APMM* 221. Plato as heir to Parmeneides: M. H. Miller Jr.,
Plato's 'Parmenides' (Princeton, NJ 1986) 28–34. 'Totally incomprehensible': E. Langlotz, *Die kulturelle und künstlerische Hellenisierung der Küsten
des Mittelmeers durch die Stadt Phokaia* (Cologne 1966) 87–8.

Parmeneides and Xenophanes: J. Burnet, *Early Greek philosophy* (4th ed., London 1930) 126–7, 170; J. Mansfeld, *Studies in the historiography of Greek philosophy* (Assen 1990) 37, 46–50; N.-L. Cordero in *Études sur le 'Sophiste' de Platon*, ed. P. Aubenque (Naples 1991) 93–124; G. Cerri in *Forme di religiosità e tradizioni sapienziali in Magna Grecia*, ed. A. C. Cassio and P. Poccetti (Pisa 1995) 137–55. From guesses to certainties: *APMM* 38–9 and *Classical Quarterly* 44 (1994) 320. 'He took part ...': D.L. 9.21 = Sotion, fragment 27 (Wehrli); Diels, *Hermes* 35 (1900) 196–200; G. S. Kirk and J. E. Raven, *The Presocratic philosophers* (Cambridge 1957) 265; Burkert 28; A. Francotte in *Mélanges Ph. Marçais* (Paris 1985) 15–16.

Walking Away

'Truly sensational': M. Timpanaro Cardini, *Studi classici e orientali* 16 (1967) 172. 'Change of perspective': P. Merlan, *Kleine philosophische Schriften* (Hildesheim 1976) 10 (first published 1966). Everything is alive: DK i 226.15–16, 353.10; W. K. C. Guthrie, *A history of Greek philosophy* ii (Cambridge 1965) 69; *APMM* 230. 'Not correct': M. M. Sassi in *Atti del ventottesimo convegno di studi sulla Magna Grecia* (Taranto 1989) 258. Conservatism of Greeks in Italy: *APMM* 244 with n. 39, 314–16, 322–3. South of Velia: *Klio* 52 (1970) 133–4. In Posidonia: *American Journal of Archaeology* 87 (1983) 302–3. Further north: G. Cerri in *Forme di religiosità e tradizioni sapienziali in Magna Grecia*, ed. A. C. Cassio and P. Poccetti (Pisa 1995) 142–3. Of the Phocaean colonists: *Journal des Savants* (1968) 213; *BCH* 99 (1975) 873–5, 895; *PP* 37 (1982) 361; Cerri 144. Molpoi: *RE* Supplementband vi (1935) 509–20; A. Laumonier, *Les cultes indigènes en Carie* (Paris 1958) 554–5; A. Brelich, *Paides e parthenoi* i (Rome 1969) 447–8, 464; *Der Kleine Pauly* iii (1975) 1402–3; F. Graf, *Museum Helveticum* 36 (1979) 2–22 and *Nordionische Kulte* (Rome 1985) 219, 415–17. Istria: D. M. Pippidi in *Stêlê: tomos eis mnêmên Nikolaou Kontoleontos* (Athens 1980) 40. Philosophy and magic: *APMM* 49–68, 217–391.

Ameinias

Wealth and social standing of priests of Apollo: S. Lambrino, *Archaiologikê Ephêmeris* (1937) 356–7; D. M. Pippidi in *Stêlê: tomos eis mnêmên Nikolaou Kontoleontos* (Athens 1980) 41–2.

Heroes and hero-shrines: Burkert, *Greek religion* (Oxford 1985) 203–8. In Pythagorean tradition: A. Delatte, *La Vie de Pythagore de Diogène*

Laërce (Brussels 1922) 227–30; P. Boyancé, *Le culte des Muses chez les philosophes grecs* (Paris 1936) 233–47; F. Cumont, *Recherches sur le symbolisme funéraire des Romains* (Paris 1942) 263; M. Detienne, *Revue de l'histoire des religions* 158 (1960) 19–53, *Homère, Hésiode et Pythagore* (Brussels 1962) 82–93 and *La notion de daïmôn dans le Pythagorisme ancien* (Paris 1963); *Kotinos: Festschrift für Erika Simon* (Mainz am Rhein 1992) 278, 326; *APMM* 250–77. Hero-shrines and silence: O. Casel, *De philosophorum Graecorum silentio mystico* (Giessen 1919) 23; Burkert, *Greek religion* 208. *Hêsychia* and silence: D.L. 8.7 and 10; Plutarch, *Moral essays* 728d; Lucian, *Lives for sale* 3; Casel 23, 26 n., 61, 75, 115–16; A. Dieterich, *Eine Mithrasliturgie* (3rd ed., Leipzig 1923) 229.

Hero-shrines and incubation: Rohde 132–3; Deubner 6, 56–7; S. Eitrem, *RE* viii/1 (1912) 1114–16; W. R. Halliday, *Greek divination* (London 1913) 128–9; L. R. Farnell, *Greek hero cults and ideas of immortality* (Oxford 1921) 239; A. Brelich, *Gli eroi greci* (Rome 1958) 107–11, 113–15. And Christian saints: Rohde 151; Deubner 56–134; N. Fernandez Marcos, *Los Thaumata de Sofronio: contribución al estudio de la incubatio cristiana* (Madrid 1975); Burkert, *Greek religion* 207. Across the mountain from Acharaca: Strabo, *Geography* 14.1.45.

Stillness, Greek philosophy, India: Timon, fragment 67 (Diels); E. Flintoff, *Phronesis* 25 (1980) 88–108. *Hêsychia* and healing: Plutarch, *Aemilius Paulus* 39; Iamblichus, *The Pythagorean life* 64–5, 196–7. And Apollo: Pindar, *Pythian odes* 4.294–6; Philochorus, fragment 170 (Jacoby); C. Schefer, *Platon und Apollon* (Sankt Augustin 1996) 173–4. Pythagoreans and stillness: Cicero, *On divination* 1.30.62; Lucian, *Lives for sale* 3; Hippolytus, *Refutation of all heresies* 1.2.18; D.L. 8.7, 10, 31–2; Iamblichus, *Pythagorean life* 10, 65, 114, 197; Delatte 224–5; H. Gomperz, *Psychologische Beobachtungen an griechischen Philosophen* (Vienna 1924) 3 n. 5; A.-J. Festugière, *Revue des études grecques* 58 (1945) 48 n. 2; Detienne, *Notion de daïmôn* 71–9; M. Marcovich, *Estudios de filosofia griega* i (Merida 1965) 14; Burkert 28 and *LS* 155 n. 197; A. H. Coxon, *The fragments of Parmenides* (Assen 1986) 38; A. Francotte in *Mélanges Ph. Marçais* (Paris 1985) 18–19; *APMM* 283–6. 'In deep meditation ...': Delatte 224. *Phôleos* and *hêsychia*: Strabo 14.1.44; Galen, *Prognosis from pulses* 1 (*PP* 35, 1980, 247); Aelian, *Nature of animals* 3.10.7; Porphyry, *To Gaurus* 1.3.

Parmeneides and stillness: DK § 28 B1.29, B8; Plato, *Parmenides* 139a–b (... *hêsychian* ...), 162d–e (... *hêsychian* ...); J. Helderman, *Die Anapausis im Evangelium Veritatis* (Leiden 1984) 59–60; L. Brisson, *Platon: Parménide* (Paris 1994) 64.

Like the Wind at Night

Stillness as inhuman and divine: E. R. Dodds, *Euripides: Bacchae* (2nd ed., Oxford 1960) xliv, 154. *Pythagorean Memoirs*: D.L. 8.31–3 (*... kath' hautên ... êremêi ... mantikên te pasan ... êremein ...*); A. Delatte, *La Vie de Pythagore de Diogène Laërce* (Brussels 1922) 224–5 (*... mantikê ...*); A.-J. Festugière, *Revue des études grecques* 58 (1945) 48 n. 2 (*... kath' heautên ... promanteuetai ...*). Stillness impossible for humans, reserved for divine beings: DK § 28 B6, B16 (*... hekastot' ... polyplanktôn ...*); Alexander Polyhistor in D.L. 8.32; Timon, fragment 67.2–5 (Diels); Iamblichus, *The Pythagorean life* 10–11; Delatte 229. Pythagorean teaching methods: *APMM* 230–2, 299, 359–70. And riddles: ibid., 42–5, 360–3 with n. 12, 371–2, 375–6; *Parabola* 22/1 (1997) 21–2.

Playing with Toys

'Assolutamente sicura': letter from Mario Napoli to Hans Jucker, published in *Museum Helveticum* 25 (1968) 183. Parmeneides' head: ibid., 181–5; Fabbri–Trotta 97, 102–4; F. Krinzinger, *Römische Historische Mitteilungen* 29 (1987) 26 and in *Velia: Studi e ricerche*, ed. G. Greco and Krinzinger (Modena 1994) 54 n. 83; K. Schefold, *Die Bildnisse der antiken Dichter, Redner und Denker* (2nd ed., Basle 1997) 230–1, 474, 512–13 (inaccurate). Athens in the ancient world: Kingsley (1995) 185–91; *APMM* 9–10, 149–60, 296, 339–41. 'To contribute to destroying ...': Thucydides, *History* 8.26; *APMM* 152. 'He had a greater love ...': D.L. 9.28 (*... ta polla ...*) with Plutarch, *Pericles* 7.2 and 27.4 (*... ta polla ...*); K. J. Dover, *Talanta* 7 (1976) 38. Plainness and austerity of Velia, Phocaea, Marseilles: J.-P. Morel, *PP* 21 (1966) 402–3 n. 78 and 37 (1982) 489–90, *BCH* 99 (1975) 856; S. Bakhuisen in *Le Pont-Euxin vu par les Grecs*, ed. O. Lordkipanidzé and P. Lévêque (Paris 1990) 57. Fictional dialogue in Plato's time: C. H. Kahn, *Plato and the Socratic dialogue* (Cambridge 1996) 34–5. Symbolism of the *Parmenides*: H. Corbin in H. Stierlin, *Ispahan* (Lausanne 1976) 1–10. Parmeneides and Zeno as ambassadors and negotiators of peace: E. Lepore, *PP* 21 (1966) 270–8; V. Panebianco, *PP* 25 (1970) 62.

The Lawgivers

Parmeneides and Zeno as lawgivers: Speusippus, fragment 3 (Tarán) = D.L. 9.23 ('He gave laws ...'); Strabo, *Geography* 6.1.1; Plutarch, *Moral essays* 1126a–b; E. L. Minar, Jr., *American Journal of Philology* 70 (1949)

44–6; L. Tarán, *Parmenides* (Princeton, NJ 1965) 5; P. Merlan, *Kleine philosophische Schriften* (Hildesheim 1976) 10; M. M. Sassi in *Atti del ventottesimo convegno di studi sulla Magna Grecia* (Taranto 1989) 257; J.-P. Morel in *Le Pont-Euxin vu par les Grecs*, ed. O. Lordkipanidzé and P. Lévêque (Paris 1990) 16. Plato's nephew: Merlan 132; K. von Fritz, *Platon in Sizilien* (Berlin 1968) 72, 133–4; *LS* 47; *APMM* 177.

Apollo and lawgiving: H. Vos, *Themis* (Assen 1956) 20–1; G. R. Morrow, *Plato's Cretan city* (Princeton, NJ 1960) 409–10; M. Detienne, *Les maîtres de vérité dans la Grèce archaïque* (Paris 1967) 29–33, 43; *Der Neue Pauly* i (1996) 867. Molpoi as ambassadors and negotiators of peace: G. Kawerau and A. Rehm, *Das Delphinion in Milet* (Berlin 1914) 286–381; *Hermes* 65 (1930) 169; *Museum Helveticum* 36 (1979) 7–8. The man from Sicily: *APMM* (Empedocles). The four vocations: DK § 31 B146; A. D. Nock and A.-J. Festugière, *Corpus hermeticum* iv (Paris 1954) 13 § 42; G. Zuntz, *Persephone* (Oxford 1971) 232–4; *APMM* 343–6.

Priests 'of Apollo and the Sun': Plato, *Laws* 945e–947b. Worshipped as heroes: ibid., 947b–e. The Pythagorean origins: P. Boyancé, *Le culte des Muses chez les philosophes grecs* (Paris 1936) 269–71 and in *Mélanges Carcopino* (Paris 1966) 163–4; Detienne, *La notion de daïmôn dans le Pythagorisme ancien* (Paris 1963) 116; Plato, *Laws* 947b5–6 with Plato, *Phaedo* 117e1–2 ('I have heard ...') and *APMM* 104–5, 108–9, 162–3 ('I have heard'), Iamblichus, *The Pythagorean life* 257 ('... caused offence to people in general without exception because it was realized that what they were doing was unique to them alone ...'), Damascius, *On Plato's 'Phaedo'* 1.559 and 2.155 ('Pythagoreans'), Boyancé, *Culte* 136–8. Plato and Pythagoreans: *LS* 84; *APMM*.

Apollo, lawgiving, and the building of hero-shrines: Plato, *Republic* 427b–c ('... If we know ...') and *Laws* 738b–d; M. Lombardo, *Annali della Scuola Normale Superiore di Pisa, Classe di lettere e filosofia*, Series 3, 2/1 (1972) 77–8. The visions or inspiration: Plato, *Laws* 738b–d; Boyancé, *Culte* 52–3 n.; Lombardo 78. Lawgiving and dreams in southern Italy: Aristotle, fragments 553 and 555 (Gigon); Plutarch, *Moral essays* 543a; H. Thesleff, *The Pythagorean texts of the Hellenistic period* (Åbo 1965) 225–9; F. Costabile, *I Ninfei di Locri Epizefiri* (Catanzaro 1991) 189–90 (Zaleucus). Revelation, lawgivers and Parmeneides: M. L. West, *Hesiod, Theogony* (Oxford 1966) 159–60.

The Night Gathering: Plato, *Laws* 951d–e, 961a–969d; Morrow 500–15; B. Vancamp, *Revue belge de philologie et d'histoire* 71 (1993) 80–4; C. Schefer, *Platon und Apollon* (Sankt Augustin 1996) 213–16. 'He would get up at night ...': *Tragicorum Graecorum fragmenta* iii, ed. S. Radt (Göttingen 1985) 138–9; West, *Studies in Aeschylus* (Stuttgart 1990)

34–5. Plato's reuse of myth: *APMM* 101–3, 108–9, 195–203, 208–11, 256, 296, 340.

Justice, laws and the cave of Night: O. Kern, *Orphicorum fragmenta* (Berlin 1922) 168–9 § 105 (... *nomothetousa* ...); West, *The Orphic poems* (Oxford 1983) 72–3, 109–10, 124, 213–14.

Epimenides at Athens: Plutarch, *Solon* 12 (... *nomothesias* ... *dikaiou* ...) and D.L. 1.110; H. Demoulin, *Épiménide de Crète* (Brussels 1901) 109–11; J. Bouffartigue and M. Patillon, *Porphyre: De l'abstinence* ii (Paris 1979) 207; G. Camassa in *Les savoirs de l'écriture*, ed. M. Detienne (Lille 1988) 144–6.

Cretan incubation and lawgiving: Detienne, *Maîtres de vérité* 38–9, 42–50, 129–31. Incubation, healing and laws: Iamblichus, *On the mysteries* 3.3. Cretan *kouros* traditions, Miletus and Phocaea: F. Graf, *Museum Helveticum* 36 (1979) 19–20 and *Nordionische Kulte* (Rome 1985) 416–17.

Javânmard and *fatâ*: H. Corbin, *En Islam iranien* iv (Paris 1972) 178, 410–30 and *L'homme et son ange* (Paris 1983) 207–60; J. Baldick in *Annali dell'Istituto Universitario Orientale di Napoli* 50 (1990) 345–61. From early Greek philosophy to the East: *APMM* 2, 49–68, 217–391. 'The traces ... corrupted and distorted': al-Shahrazûrî in Shihâb al-Dîn Yahyâ al-Suhrawardî, *Opera metaphysica et mystica* ii, ed. H. Corbin (Tehran 1952) 5–6; *APMM* 387. Early Greek philosophers in Sufism and Persian mysticism: Corbin, *Spiritual body and celestial earth* (Princeton, NJ 1977) 171; *APMM* 375–91. In Arab alchemy: P. Lory, *Ğâbir ibn Ḥayyân, L'élaboration de l'élixir suprême* (Damascus 1988) 14–18 with 15 n. 33; Kingsley (1994a); *APMM* 56–68, 375–9, 387–90.

A Matter of Practicalities

'There is not the slightest indication': Mourelatos 45. 'That human beings ... undistinguishing crowds': DK § 28 B6.4–7. 'Ordinary' mortals 'who only see ...': W. J. Verdenius, *Parmenides* (Groningen 1942) 56.

The Pythagorean and Parmenidean way of life: *Cebes' tablet* 2. Our lives as a riddle: ibid., 3; J. T. Fitzgerald and L. M. White, *The Tabula of Cebes* (Chico, CA 1983) 137. Pythagoreans and practicality: *APMM* 157–8, 335–47. 'Philosophy' and Pythagoreans: C. J. de Vogel, *Philosophia* i (Assen 1970) 81–2; *APMM* 339–41. Their coining of new words: de Vogel, *Pythagoras and early Pythagoreanism* (Assen 1966) 136, 218–20. Plato's host: *APMM* 94–5, 144–8, 156–7, 164. Pythagoreans and warfare: ibid., 143–58.

Zeno's death: DK § 29 A1–2, 6–9, with O. Casel, *De philosophorum Graecorum silentio mystico* (Giessen 1919) 56; E. L. Minar, Jr., *American Journal of Philology* 70 (1949) 44–5; P. J. Bicknell in *For service to classical studies: essays in honour of Francis Letters*, ed. M. Kelly (Melbourne 1966) 10–14; G. Calogero, *Studi sull'eleatismo* (2nd ed., Florence 1977) 106 n. 2; T. Dorandi in *Ainsi parlaient les anciens: in honorem Jean-Paul Dumont* (Lille 1994) 27–37. 'He tested …': Plutarch, *Moral essays* 1126d. The historical background: L. Bernabò Brea, *PP* 37 (1982) 371–3; G. Manganaro, *Chiron* 22 (1992) 386 n. 5 (Oulis), 390–1. Fighting against Athens: *PP* 21 (1966) 270–8 and 25 (1970) 62–3.

ACKNOWLEDGEMENTS

to Hirmer Fotoarchiv in Munich for permission to reproduce the image on the front cover

to Van Gorcum in Assen for the detail from the oldest known manuscript that preserves the start of Parmenides' poem (p. 48)

and to Giorgio Bretschneider Editore in Rome for the pictures of the Parmeneides inscription (p. 138) and the matching head (p. 194)

Introducing the sequel to IN THE DARK PLACES OF WISDOM

REALITY
(Catafalque Press 2020, www.catafalquepress.com)

"*Reality* contains the purest and most powerful writing I have ever read."
Michael Baigent, author of *Ancient Traces* and *The Holy Blood and the Holy Grail*

"Peter Kingsley is a successor to Carl Jung and Joseph Campbell. His lectures and writings—especially his latest book, *Reality*—reveal hidden dimensions of consciousness and how it manifests in the world. His message conveys hope and meaning, and reveals majestic qualities of the mind we have forgotten and which have been ignored by Western 'authorities' for centuries. Peter Kingsley is a transformative and life-changing force in our world. Never have we needed such a message as now."
Larry Dossey, M.D., author of *Healing Beyond the Body* and *Reinventing Medicine*

"Dr. Kingsley's remarkable new book, *Reality*, is extraordinarily valuable. It would be difficult not to conclude that, through his research into our past, he has found the key to the modern world impasse."
Robert A. Johnson, author of *He, She, Inner Work,*
and *Balancing Heaven and Earth*

"Stunningly original, *Reality* is momentous in its implications."
Huston Smith, author of *The World's Religions* and *Forgotten Truth*

A STORY WAITING TO PIERCE YOU
MONGOLIA, TIBET AND THE DESTINY OF THE WESTERN WORLD
(The Golden Sufi Center 2010)

"In this profoundly erudite and eloquent book is a startling ancient secret that will forever alter the way we think about the origins of western civilization."
Pir Zia Inayat Khan

"By challenging some of our most fundamental perceptions of early European history, Peter Kingsley pushes out the horizon of the modern world and opens a new chapter in our appreciation of European–Asian relations. His innovative research into the spiritual and intellectual debt of ancient Greece to Inner Asia not only broadens our understanding of the past, but also helps us to understand better who we are today."
Jack Weatherford, author of *Genghis Khan and the Making of the Modern World*

"I have read *A Story Waiting to Pierce You* with tremendous fascination. It is a unique work—a captivating and enlightening book which I heartily recommend to anyone with an interest in Eurasian history."
Victor Mair, author of *Secrets of the Silk Road* and *The Tarim Mummies*

CATAFALQUE

(Catafalque Press 2018: www.catafalquepress.com)

"In this remarkable study, Peter Kingsley engages with a question Carl Jung describes as the most telling of one's life: 'Are you related to something infinite or not?' Written in an 'ancient style', 'the choiceless rhythm of the winds and rain', *Catafalque* is an extraordinary achievement—demonstrating an impressively broad cultural knowledge coupled with an impeccable attention to detail. In its focus on Jung as a mystic and as a magician, it not only confirms Spinoza's thesis that we feel and know we are eternal; it will also provoke and charm the reader by turns."

Prof. Paul Bishop, University of Glasgow, author of *Carl Jung* and *On the Blissful Islands with Nietzsche and Jung*

"Here at last is the true Jung: the Jung whom those who dare to call themselves Jungians have forgotten and betrayed, a Jung who often is far too frightening to be understood. Nothing could be less comforting than this Jung or less comfortable than this book—pointing as they do to the extraordinary failure of western civilization to return to its roots, pay respect to its ancestors, listen to its dead. Deeply researched, challenging at every turn, I couldn't put *Catafalque* down."

Maggy Anthony, author of *Salome's Embrace* and *Jung's Circle of Women*

"For all its scholarly precision, and artistic sophistication, *Catafalque* is a dangerous book. But numinous truths are often dangerous even to behold, much more to write about. And if you can summon the courage to open your eyes where Peter's magic takes you, you might get a glimpse of a long lost part of our collective soul."

Adyashanti, author of *Emptiness Dancing* and *The End of Your World*

"I had known nothing of Jung until this book appeared and I see now that one is indeed in front of unknowns, imponderables, unfathomable mysteries. This compelling book is an absolute eye-opener, a wonderful gift. In *Catafalque* Peter Kingsley brings together an extraordinary set of credentials: a body of unequalled scholarship, literary skills which are second to none, and a rare grasp of the living nature of things that lies beyond the constructs of our thought. In his unique regard both for the real or transcendent and for the delicate and ephemeral, he is a servant of the Lord indeed."

Frank Sinclair, President emeritus of the Gurdjieff Foundation, New York, author of *Without Benefit of Clergy* and *Of the Life Aligned*

"Peter Kingsley writes with the force of a sorcerer, which is also what he is writing about. He is an author of the impossible. Perhaps some day I will know the place from which he expresses himself. I have sought it my entire life."

Prof. Jeffrey Kripal, Rice University, Houston, author of *Secret Body* and *Super Natural*